Powerful Passages

*True stories of people whose lives
were changed by a single scripture*

Ron and Dorothy Watts

Pacific Press Publishing Association
Boise, Idaho
Oshawa, Ontario, Canada

Edited by Jerry D. Thomas
Designed by Dennis Ferree
Cover illustration by Thomas Duckworth
Typeset in 14/17 Caslon 224 Book

The accuracy of all facts and quoted material is the
responsibility of the authors.

ISBN 0-8163-1337-7

96 97 98 99 00 • 5 4 3 2 1

Contents

Introduction

pow•er•ful: Having much power, potent; strong, mighty; influential, consequential; capable, effective; authoritative; forceful, dynamic; vigorous, energetic; cogent, compelling.[1]

All of these meanings of the word *powerful* apply to the Word of God. So potent are the words of Scripture that through one sentence God can change drunkards into deacons and head hunters into angels of mercy. One phrase of Scripture has caused men to completely change careers and has enabled fearful women to become courageous workers for God.

The true stories in this book are proof that the Bible is capable of transforming not only the character of a person, but his appearance as well. So dynamic is God's Word that one verse has tamed the vilest temper, healed the deepest hurts, and prevented suicide.

The forty stories in this book demonstrate the life-changing power there is in one verse of Scripture. Each tells of the impact of the Bible on the life of a famous person. Some are well-known contemporaries, but others, famous a century or two ago, have now been all but forgotten. However, all have compelling stories to tell of how one passage worked a miracle in their lives.

The channel of God's power

"The word of God—the truth—is the channel through which the Lord manifests His Spirit and power." [2]

In the spring of 1841, George Muller discovered the power there is in a passage of Scripture. Before this time, he regularly prayed to God before he dressed in the morning, but he was not experiencing the complete power and happiness of the Christian life. During a holiday in the country, he felt impressed to give himself to the study of God's Word.

He wrote in his journal, "Now I saw that the most important thing I had to do was to give myself to the reading of the Word of God, and to meditation on it, that thus my heart might be comforted, encouraged, warned, reproved, instructed; and that thus, by means of the Word of God, wilst meditating upon it, my heart might be brought into experimental communion with the Lord." [3]

Muller began a systematic study of the New Testament in the early morning hours, meditating on each verse, seeking a blessing from it. About its transforming power he wrote, "The result I have found to be almost invariably this . . . by breakfast time, with rare exceptions, I am in a peaceful if not happy state of heart."[4]

The Bible is not an ordinary book. Bibles are frequently printed on fine India paper and bound with expensive leather. But the Bible is much more than black ink on fine paper! It is a living book! It is a life-giving book!

Hebrews 4:12 declares, "The word of God is living and powerful . . ." (NKJV). No, the Bible itself does not have magical power, but when the word of God is received into the mind and heart through the agency of Scripture, it can have a powerful life-changing impact.

The ancient poet declared, "The entrance of Your words gives light" (Psalm 119:130, NKJV). Peter claimed that the Word of God was so effective that it caused people to be born again (see 1 Peter 1:23).

The power connection

The overseas missionary had a problem. He had the use of the mission car, but it wouldn't start. He decided he needed a push, so he went to the mission school nearby and asked if some of the boys could help him push the car.

In no time, the motor was chugging, and he was on his way to town to do mission business. At the first stop, he parked the car on a hill so gravity could help him get restarted.

At the next place, he left the engine running. For two years the frugal missionary used this system with the old car that wouldn't start.

Then a new missionary arrived, and the old car was allotted to him. Proudly, the old missionary explained his arrangement for getting the car started. The new arrival looked under the hood.

"Here's your trouble, Brother," the man said, pointing to a loose cable. With a few twists, it was in place. "Now give it a try," he said.

To the old missionary's astonishment, the engine roared to life! "And to think that it was only a loose connection," he said. "Even I could have fixed that!"[5]

Tremendous power—God's mighty life-changing power—is available to anyone who makes the connection with God through His Word. This book is the story of forty men and women who made that connection.

How to use this book

1. Read the story and marvel at the power of God's living Word at work in a human life. Catch a little of the awe the person must have felt when he recognized God's voice speaking to him.

2. Read the Epilogue to learn more about that famous

person. As you read of his or her achievements, you will begin to understand the far-reaching effect of Scripture on that person's life and work.

3. If you want to know more about the individual who has experienced a life-changing encounter with the Word, turn to the reference section for the source of more information on that person's life.

4. After our use of these experiences in sermons or seminars, people have often asked for copies they might use in their own ministry. Good stories get better as they are shared. After reading the story for each powerful passage, you will want to share it! Use it for family worship; incorporate it into a church program; use it as a sermon illustration; tell it to your study class; include it in a vesper program; share it in your prayer group; call some shut-ins, and give them a powerful passage story to brighten their day!

5. Memorize the powerful passage. Our experience has shown that connecting a text with the story of how it worked in someone's life helps fix the text in the memory.

6. Meditate on the powerful passage. Read it from several versions. Ask the Lord to speak His specific message to you through the same text. Take the verse and concentrate on finding the thought which God has put there for you. If we dwell on the thought until it becomes our own, we will know 'what saith the Lord.'

God can use these texts to transform your life, just as

POWERFUL PASSAGES

He has changed the lives of the men and women in these stories. What He's done for them, He will gladly do for you.

**"The Word of God is living and powerful."
Hebrews 4:12, NKJV.**

1.The Random House Dictionary of the English Language, Second Edition, Unabriged (New York: Random House) 1966, 1517.
2. Ellen G. White, *The Desire of Ages* (Boise, Idaho: Pacific Press Publishing Assoc., 1940), 520.
3. Roger Steer, "Seeking First the Kingdom: The Secret of George Muller's Spiritual Peace," *Discipleship Journal*, 1985, 31:25
4. Ibid.
5. Craig Brian Larson, ed., *Illustrations for Preaching and Teaching* (Grand Rapids, Mich.: Baker Books, 1993),182.

*hoose you this day
whom ye will serve.*

Joshua 24:15

A Man of Courage

It was April 21, 1908. The ice was already breaking up, and Dr. Wilfred Grenfell knew it was chancy, but there was no one else to make the trip. Someone across a Labrador bay needed the services of a doctor, and that is what he believed God had called him to Labrador to provide.

He set off with his dog team across the treacherous ice hoping that he might make it. But the wind suddenly changed direction, and Grenfell found himself helplessly adrift on an ice pan, heading for the open sea. His cap, jacket, and all his supplies had been lost in the scramble to get on the ice pan. He realized death was almost certain, as rescue seemed impossible.

However, Grenfell was not there for his own pleasure

or profit. He knew that God wanted him to live, and he believed that he must do everything in his power to survive. Then came a time of difficult decision.

He loved his sled dogs. They had given him faithful and devoted service, but he could not survive long without clothes. He made the decision. Selecting three of the dogs and turning his back to the others, Grenfell killed and skinned them, making primitive clothing for himself.

He then took leather thongs and joined the leg bones of the dead dogs to make a pole. He hung his shirt from that pole and though fatigued and hungry, regularly waved that flag. He hoped and prayed that someone would see it and come to his rescue. Frostbitten and cold, he determined to wait and hope. Eventually, he was seen and rescued.

In his autobiography, Dr. Grenfell tells how, in the dark, lonesome hours on the ice pan, the words of an old hymn kept running through his head, giving him courage and strength.

> "My God, my Father, while I stray,
> Far from my home on life's rough way,
> Oh, help me from my heart to say,
> Thy will be done."

That wasn't the first time Dr. Wilfred Grenfell chose to make a difficult, life-changing decision. In fact, he would never have gone as a missionary doctor to Newfoundland were it not for a decision he had made twenty-five years before.

One evening in 1883, he was going down a dark street in London, England, to visit a maternity case. He saw a crowd gathering in a large tent and, out of curiosity, went inside to see what was happening.

Dwight L. Moody, the shoe-salesman-turned-evangelist, was conducting a public evangelistic meeting. An old man was in the midst of a very long prayer. Bored, Grenfell almost left. Just then, energetic Moody jumped up and called out to the audience, "While our brother finishes his prayer, let us sing a song!"

The humor of that incident caught Grenfell's attention. He listened to Moody's sermon and went away convinced that religion was something much more challenging than he had ever thought it to be. Following that encounter, Grenfell started to read the Bible to see if it was the guide to life that he had been seeking.

Some time later, a group of well-known Christian athletes held an event in East London. They were cricketers and oarsmen of international fame. Known as the "Cambridge Seven," all were about to go as missionaries to China. Their leaders were Charles Studd, British cricket hero, and S. P. Smith, champion oarsman.

The seven had social prestige, wealth, and sporting prowess. All seven volunteered to do missionary service with the China Inland Mission. This made a major impact on the youth of Britain, including Wilfred Grenfell.

Smith spoke on the appeal of Joshua, "Choose ye this day whom ye will serve." He noted that you can serve self from fear of comrades and others, or you can serve Christ. Then he made an appeal for all those who decided to serve Christ to stand to their feet.

Grenfell knew Smith was right but felt chained by fear to his seat. At that moment, a young naval recruit stood up before more than a hundred of his comrades. The example of that youth's courage gave Grenfell courage to do the same.

Writing about that night, Grenfell said, "This step I have ever since been thankful for. . . . It entirely changed the meaning of life to me."

Epilogue

In 1892, Grenfell sailed for Newfoundland's Labrador coast to explore the living conditions. He found much beriberi, tuberculosis, and other illnesses and no doctors available to treat the people. In three months, he saw 900 patients.

Dr. Wilfred Grenfell spent forty years serving the medical needs of these people, who lived in primitive conditions.

In 1899, he was given a hospital ship, the *Strathcona*. In 1927, he was knighted by King George V.

Grenfell wrote twenty-four books, established five hospitals, and set up seven nursing stations. He also opened orphanages, churches, and schools. He improved the lot of Eskimos, native Indians, and whites by opening cooperative stores and teaching improved methods of seal fishing and fox farming.

In 1912, Grenfell opened the Seaman's Institute of St. John's, Newfoundland. He retired in 1935 to Charlotte, Vermont, where he died five years later, after forty years of trying to put Christianity into action.

About him, one admirer said, "If Wilfred Grenfell came through that door now I would feel that Jesus Christ had entered the room." More than half a century after his death, he is still remembered with love by people along the rugged coasts of Labrador.

The Lord, he is the God;
the Lord, he is the God.

1 Kings 18:39

God's Last Chance

It was July 1924. Nineteen-year-old Hannah had come to Keswick at the urging of her father to give God one last chance. She attended two meetings a day according to the bargain she had made with him. The rest of the time she roamed the countryside thinking.

God, where are You? Why don't You speak to me? Maybe Christianity is all a delusion, Hannah's heart cried out.

Friday morning there was a final meeting. However, it was different from the others. There was no preaching. Twelve missionaries testified of God's power. It seemed to Hannah that their faces shone with the brightness of heaven. For three hours she sat, fascinated with the stories of daily miracles.

Hannah thought, *There must be a God—one who is willing to speak to everyone but me. Why can't I find Him?* The testimonies finished, and the leader made an altar call. Hundreds went forward, but Hannah could not. She ran from the tent to the privacy of her room and fell to her knees beside her bed. "God, if You are there, please speak to me. If You don't reveal yourself I shall know there is no hope anywhere in the universe."

Reaching for her Bible, she challenged the Almighty, "Okay, God. Here's Your chance. Speak to me through Your Word."

The Bible fell open to 1 Kings 18. How could God speak in a book of military history? She was tempted to close the Bible but decided it wouldn't hurt to read it. With little hope of finding Him, she began to read the story of Elijah challenging the false prophets of Baal. She read how God consumed the sacrifice.

God is asking me to make a sacrifice too, Hannah suddenly realized. *He wants me to give Him all that I have, to be willing to witness for Him, maybe even to be a missionary!*

The words of verse 21 spoke to her heart. "How long halt ye between two opinions? If the Lord be God, follow Him."

After several agonizing moments, Hannah cried out, "If You will make Yourself real to me and help me, I will give You my stammering tongue, and I will become a missionary."

Opening her eyes, Hannah read the words in verse

39, "The Lord, He is the God; the Lord, He is the God." Suddenly it seemed that her heart was filled with a warm, glorious light. She felt two loving arms around her and heard a voice whisper tenderly, "Here I am, Hannah. I have been here all the time, but you locked yourself away from the consciousness of My presence by refusing to yield yourself completely. I love you. I will never leave you."

Epilogue

Hannah attended Bible college, then traveled with the Friends' Evangelistic Band of itinerant evangelists in Ireland and England for four years. She later became a missionary to Palestine, where most of her life was spent working for the Jews. She died in 1990.

The story of Hannah Hurnard's walk with God is found in her book *Hind's Feet on High Places*, a Christian classic.

The judgments of the Lord
are true and righteous altogether.
Psalm 19:9

Gettysburg Surrender

Fifteen months before Robert E. Lee capitulated the confederacy to Ulysses S. Grant at Appomattox, the commander in chief, Abraham Lincoln, made his surrender to the commander of heaven on the field of Gettysburg.

When Abe Lincoln was elected president of the United States in 1861, it was with less than 40 per cent of the popular vote. More people voted against him than voted for him.

Even before he arrived in Washington, every mail delivery brought death threats. Close friends advised him to resign before taking the oath of office. A plot to assassinate the president-elect was uncovered on his way to Washington, and the last leg of that trip was made in the dead of night in secret under heavy guard.

Before his inauguration, seven states seceded from the union, and a secessionist government was established.

Lincoln's views on slavery were widely published throughout the nation during his debates with Douglas two years before. He declared slavery morally, socially, and politically wrong.

Now his enemies were afraid he would use his influence as president to outlaw slavery. But there were many who believed God had brought him to high office for this very purpose. Lincoln believed both views wrong. He was of the view that his responsibility as president was to preserve the Union, not abolish slavery. However, as the blood began to flow and northern armies lost battle after battle, Lincoln began to wonder if that cause was just and whether or not God was punishing the nation for the terrible institution of slavery.

Lincoln had been taught by his natural mother, Nancy Lincoln, to respect God and read the Bible. She often read to him as a child from the family Bible. She died when he was nine, but he remembered her last words to him, "Love your heavenly Father and keep His commandments."

His stepmother took him to the local Baptist Church on many occasions, and he himself spent many hours reading the King James Version of the Bible. But by his own testimony, he was not a practicing Christian when he entered the White House.

Lincoln felt deeply the agony of the nation as the flower of her youth were being swallowed by the thousands in the bloodshed and misery of the war. He wept openly when reports from the front brought news of the awful loss of life that was daily occurring.

Then his sorrow was deepened by a terrible personal tragedy. His youngest son, Willie, the apple of the president's eye, died suddenly in the White House. Both he and his wife were inconsolable in their grief.

Willie's nurse shared with the president her very personal relationship with Jesus Christ. She encouraged him to trust in Jesus as his personal Saviour. He did not at that time respond.

Shortly after that, Lincoln decided that God had allowed this terrible war to bring about the abolition of slavery. He promised God that if He would give the Union an important victory, Lincoln would issue an emancipation proclamation.

That September, Lee crossed the Potomac into Maryland. Providentially, his secret orders to divide his troops came into possession of the union commander, General McClellan, and the ferocious Battle of Sharpsburg, near Antietam Creek, took place. The casualties at Antietam totalled four times more than those suffered by American soldiers on the beaches of Normandy in June 1944. Lee retreated into Virginia. Lincoln, feeling his prayer was answered, issued the preliminary Proclamation of Emancipation.

Fourteen months later, at the dedication of a cemetery at Gettysburg, Abraham Lincoln, the president of the United States, finally made his personal surrender in faith to Jesus Christ.

He later told a friend, "When I left Springfield, I asked the people to pray for me; I was not a Christian. When I buried my son—the severest trial of my life—I was not a Christian. But when I went to Gettysburg and saw the graves of thousands of our soldiers, I then and there consecrated myself to Christ." He shared with friends with deep emotion that he had at last found peace.

Following this, he worshiped regularly at the New York Avenue Presbyterian Church, both on Sunday and at Wednesday evening prayer meetings. He told the pastor of the church that he wanted to become a member and make a public confession of his faith in Christ.

This faith and surrender comes through very clearly in his second inaugural address given a few months later. It contains fourteen references to God and a reference to Psalm 19:9, that powerfully expresses his own surrender to the will of God in the midst of the terrible tragedy of war.

He said, "Fondly do we hope—fervently do we pray—that this mighty scourge of war may speedily pass away. Yet, if God wills that it continue, until all the wealth piled by the bondsman's two hundred and fifty years of unrequited toil shall be sunk, and until every drop of blood drawn with the lash shall be paid by another drawn with the sword, as was said three thousand years ago, so still it must be said, 'the judgments of the Lord are true and righteous altogether.' "

Previously, as the war dragged on, he questioned the judgments of God. Now having made his surrender, he declared the judgments of God completely justified.

Epilogue

This second inaugural address was delivered on March 15, 1865. On April 9, General Robert E. Lee surrendered at the Court House in Appomattox, Virginia, bringing an end to the American Civil War. On April 14, Abraham Lincoln was shot by John Wilkes Booth, an actor, and died the next morning. He had effectively brought about what may be the greatest achievement of the nineteenth century, the legal abolition of slavery.

Trust in the Lord, and do good;
so shalt thou dwell in the land,
and verily thou shalt be fed.
Delight thyself also in the Lord;
and he shall give thee the desires of thine heart.

Psalm 37:3, 4

The Watergate Scandal

Chuck Colson was not sure why he called Tom Phillips for a second visit when he was in the Boston area, but Tom welcomed the call. Chuck himself was surprised at how much he looked forward to the meeting.

These were tough days for ex-marine Lieutenant Colson. He had joined the Nixon bandwagon in Washington and had become a White House insider. As the architect of Nixon's reelection campaign in 1972, Colson had helped win 49 of 50 states, plus the biggest margin in history. Then the Watergate scandal broke, and Colson returned disillusioned to his private law practice.

One of his new clients was the largest employer in Massachusetts, the Raytheon Company. Colson had been warned that the president, Tom Phillips, had recently been changed by a religious experience. He casually asked about it.

"Yes, I have accepted Jesus Christ and committed my life to him. This has been the most marvelous experience of my life," Phillips admitted.

What is he talking about? Chuck wondered. *How can you accept Someone who lived two thousand years ago as though He were still around today? How does a person commit his life to Christ?*

Tom continued to share. "I had gotten to the place where I felt my life was meaningless, without foundation. Now everything has changed, including my attitudes and values. Sometime, I would be happy to tell you the whole story."

So one hot, humid night, several months later, Tom and Chuck sat together on Tom's porch sipping iced tea. Tom reviewed his rapid rise to the top of one of the largest corporations in America, one with ten billions in annual sales. He was elected president at forty. To achieve this, he had worked hard—nonstop day and night.

"The prize was mine, but it didn't satisfy," Tom admitted. "Something was missing. There was a big hole in my life. I started reading the Bible looking for answers. On a business trip to New York, I wandered one night into a Billy Graham crusade at Madison Square Garden. Hearing Graham speak, I knew what was missing—Jesus Christ. So that very night, when the invitation was given, I turned over my life to Christ. Now I have a joy and satisfaction that I never knew was possible."

The talk turned to Chuck's troubles with the press over Watergate. Tom told him, "You were wrong to do those dirty tricks in the election. You could have won without them if your cause was just and God was on your side. You went too far. Your sin was pride and it made you go too far."

Chuck realized Tom was speaking the truth. Chuck saw himself as he had never seen himself before, and the picture was ugly.

Then a powerful moment came as Tom reached for his Bible and read, "Trust in the Lord, and do good; so shalt thou dwell in the land, and verily thou shalt be fed. Delight thyself also in the Lord; and He shall give thee the desires of thine heart" (Psalm 37:3, 4).

For the first time in his life, the scripture came alive for Chuck Colson. Those words *trust in the Lord* got into his heart and caused a silent explosion. *I do want to trust the Lord*, Chuck thought, *if only I could be sure. If only I knew how!*

"May I pray with you?" Tom asked.

"Sure." Chuck wasn't sure what to expect. He'd never prayed with anyone before, except for the blessing at meals.

"Please open Chuck's heart and show him the light and the way," Tom prayed openly, naturally, as though talking to a dear friend. Chuck had been used to formal prayers in church, not the intimate kind he was hearing now. "Be with him and his family." Chuck fought to hold back the wave of emotion that threatened to reveal itself in tears. As soon as the prayer was finished, he made a hasty exit.

But when he got into his car, he was gripped by the power of the testimony he had just heard. Tears blinded his eyes, and he had to stop the car not far from Tom's driveway.

With tears flowing freely, he cried out to God, "I don't know how to find You, but I'm going to try! I'm not much the way I am now, but somehow I want to give myself to You. Take me!" Over and over he repeated the words, "Take me! Take me! Take me!"

He stayed alone in the darkness of the car crying, praying, and thinking for a half hour or more. Then, for the first time in his life, Chuck felt he was not alone. Joy filled his mind. This was the beginning of the new-birth experience for Chuck Colson as he sensed that God had revealed Himself through His Word.

Epilogue

In a few weeks, Chuck's experience of faith in Christ hit the newspapers, and the writers had a great time poking fun at him. He jokes that he kept a small army of political cartoonists fed and clothed for months.

Colson spent seven months in prison on a Watergate-related charge. This experience gave him an understanding of what prisoners face without hope.

POWERFUL PASSAGES

In 1976, he began a ministry called Prison Fellowship, Inc. It has become a spiritual help to thousands behind bars and is now international in scope.

His best-selling book about his experience, *Born Again*, has led many to conversion.

reate in me a clean heart, O God;
and renew a right spirit within me.

Psalm 51:10

Letter From an Old Friend

Eleven-year-old Allen Francis Gardiner listened nervously for every bit of news from London. It was 1805, and mighty Napoleon was preparing an armada for the conquest of England. Allen was delirious with excitement when the news of Britain's victory at Trafalgar reached his ears.

Yet he was saddened to hear that his hero, Admiral Nelson, was killed in battle. Filled with deep emotion, he determined that, like his idol Lord Nelson, he would become a naval officer, patrolling the seas for freedom.

Three years later, at the age of fourteen, Gardiner was in the navy, a brutal school for boys in the early nineteenth century. He rapidly rose in the ranks, and by the age of twenty, he, too, was a hero. He captured the American frigate *Essex* in 1814 and escorted it to Portsmouth. He was promoted to lieutenant and soon to captain.

As a child, Allen had been taught by his devout mother and Christian father to love God and live an exemplary life. Within a year of his going to sea, he received a black-edged letter informing him of his mother's early death.

Gardiner's grief turned to anger and rebellion. The ties that bound him to his mother's heart were those that tied him to purity and virtue. Both were now snapped! He forsook the religion of his godly mother and allowed himself to obey his wild impulses. He bitterly ridiculed Christianity and declared Bible reading to be utter foolishness.

Then one day, he was shocked to sober thought by the sudden death of a youthful friend. Walking the streets of Portsmouth in a religious frame of mind, Allen thought to buy a Bible.

Arriving at the book shop, he saw other customers at the counter. Ashamed to be seen asking for the Book he had so viley mocked, Allen went on down the street and waited for the store to empty of customers. However, as soon as one customer left, another went in. After a long while of pacing the street, Allen got his chance. He rushed in and hurriedly bought a Bible.

For the rest of the day, Allen had but one thought on his mind, *What must the bookseller think of me!*

Not long after that, a remarkable letter came from an

elderly lady who had been a close friend of his mother's. His vessel lay at anchor in the Strait of Malacca when the mail arrived. That day was the turning point in Gardiner's life. The year was 1820, and Allen Gardiner was twenty-six years old.

"I don't want to censor; nor would I presume to lecture you," the letter began, "but for your mother's sake, please read with patience my earnest plea."

She warned Allen of the results of sin and reminded him again of how Christ came and died in the sinner's place. She then shared with him the prayer of David in Psalm 51:10, "Create in me a clean heart, O God; and renew a right spirit within me."

"A new heart is the gift of God," she explained. "None but He can create it. . . . It must be received in this life for there is no pardon or repentance after death."

In closing she wrote, "It is probable, dear Allen, that you and I will never meet again on earth . . . let me hope that we shall meet in that place where all must hope to be, clothed in the Saviour's perfect righteousness."

Allen read her letter again and again. The power of that scripture passage and her earnest appeal reached his heart. He repented and began to trust in Jesus.

About his conversion, Gardiner wrote, "After years of ingratitude, blasphemy, and rebellion, I have at last been melted! Alas, how slow and reluctant have I been to admit the heavenly Guest who stood knocking without! Nor had He ever been received had not He Himself prepared the way!"

He made a copy of the letter from his mother's friend and placed it inside his Bible. He carried it with him on all future voyages. Ever afterward, he told that receiving that letter from his mother's friend was the great turning point of his life.

Epilogue

Commander Allen Francis Gardiner later resigned his commission in the navy to become a pioneer missionary at the age of forty.

His first mission was to the Zulus of Natal in South Africa. In May 1835, he secured a treaty with Dingaan, the Zulu chieftain for the ceding of the southern half of Natal to Britain. On June 23 of the same year, he presided over a meeting of settlers who laid out the streets for Durban. Today, Durban is the largest port city in South Africa. Gardiner Street bears his name.

He later took his wife and children to South America, where he made exploratory trips into Bolivia, Chile, and Argentina to ascertain the need for mission work.

In 1844, Gardiner organized the Patagonian Missionary Society to take the gospel to the non-Christian Indians of South America. In 1850, with six other men, he sailed for Tierra del Fuego to convert the tribes living there.

Within a few months, Gardiner and his entire party died of exposure and starvation. But their deaths inspired others to successful missionary work among the aboriginals at the tip of South America.

In 1854, a schooner named *Allen Gardiner* sailed from Bristol carrying missionaries and supplies. It was the first Methodist mission ship. The new group was successful in reaching the Indian tribes.

*W*hoso findeth me findeth life,
and shall obtain favour of the Lord.
Proverbs 8:35

Running From God

For the first time in eighteen years, Genie was in church. She wouldn't have been there that day except that Ellen, a childhood friend who had now become a Christian, had insisted. "I want to show you a beautiful old window," Ellen had said. "I think you'll like it."

Genie sat in the silence and gazed at the old, misty green window high up in a vaulted corner. Light from the morning sun illuminated a cross tipped sideways on some clouds. The cross held little meaning for her, but the beauty of the window captivated her. She couldn't seem to take her eyes away. It was lovely, just as Ellen had said.

When the sermon began, Genie grew restless for a cigarette. She felt somehow out of place with her friend

Ellen praying quietly beside her. *I don't belong here,* Genie mused, *but somehow I wish I did. I wish I could experience the grace that the preacher is talking about.*

"Grace is a gift," the preacher said. "You only have to be empty to receive it. Jesus sacrificed Himself on the Cross of Calvary not only to atone for our sins but to release grace that is sufficient for anything you have to face in life. Grace is waiting for you. All you need do is reach out and receive it."

Genie sensed that the same warm, heavenly light she saw shining through the green misty window was radiating from the pastor's face as he spoke so lovingly of Jesus. When he prayed, he seemed to be on intimate terms with God, and Genie thought, *I wish I could talk to God like that!*

But when her friend went forward to participate in communion, Genie got up and left the church. Once outside, she ran to the bar of a nearby hotel where she was staying. She needed a drink to steady her nerves. It was closed until one o'clock. To make the time pass, Genie walked around the block a few times, then stood across from the church and watched the people come out.

I wonder how many of them are real Christians and how many of them just go because it is the thing to do, Genie thought. *If I became a Christian, I'd want to be a real one. I'd want to kiss His feet with the nail prints in them.*

Startled at her own thoughts, she hurried back to the

hotel and waited for the bar to open. *This is where I belong*, Genie thought as she took her place in the darkened room and lit another cigarette. The juke box was playing a current tune. *I just don't fit in over there in the church with stained glass windows and organ music.*

Genie stayed there, drinking and smoking, until nearly two o'clock, then went to her room and ordered dinner and more drinks. Ellen returned about two-thirty. She could tell at once that Genie had been drinking, but she said nothing.

"I liked your church service," Genie spoke flippantly. "And I think Jesus Christ is rather exciting. The only thing is, you're far too radical about your religion. You're too extreme. Why do I need to give up anything to become a Christian? Being God, I think Jesus Christ should do the adapting. Surely He can adapt to me better than I can adapt to Him!"

"Genie, Jesus is not going to adapt to you," Ellen replied earnestly. "Instead He wants to change you." She put on her yellow tweed coat and headed for the door.

Genie felt panic. Somehow, she knew that if Ellen left then, she would never find God, and deep inside she knew that's what she wanted more than anything else in the world. *God, please don't let her go!* Genie prayed silently.

Ellen turned and walked back to where Genie stood beside the dresser. "It won't work any other way except His way, Genie," she said. "Jesus is the Way, the Truth, and the Life. If we would follow Him, we must give up everything for Him. He is the only Way, Genie. We can only find life in Christ."

From somewhere came snatches of a text Genie had read once in Proverbs, ". . . Whoso findeth me findeth life." The power of the thought overwhelmed her. "Whoso findeth me findeth life." Could it be true? Was this the only Way to find peace?

Ellen continued, "Genie, you'd make a terrific Christian, you know!"

Genie fell back in her chair and began to cry. "Oh, God, I wish I were dead!" she sobbed.

"I wish you were, too," Ellen spoke softly. "It would be wonderful if the old Genie Price would die right now so a new one could be born."

After a long moment, Genie looked up at her friend and whispered, "OK. I guess you're right."

It seemed in that moment that all the darkness and restlessness disappeared, and Genie's heart was filled with light and peace. She smiled through her tears. Ellen took off her coat, and the two shared the quiet of Christ's presence, the beginning of Eugenia Price's walk with God, on October 2, 1949.

Epilogue

Eugenia Price began a career in radio writing and producing in 1939. Between 1950 to 1956, she wrote, produced, and directed "Unshackled." Her first devotional book was published in 1953. Her first historical novel, *Beloved Invader*, came out in 1962.

Today you will find books by Eugenia Price on the shelves of almost every Christian book store. She has written more than thirty-five books, among which are *Before the Darkness Falls* and *Bright Captivity*, based upon the lives of people who lived on St. Simons Island, her home for over thirty years.

In 1978, Eugenia received the Governor's Award in the Arts for literature.

He who is slow to anger
is better than the mighty,
and he who rules his spirit
than he who takes a city (RSV).
Proverbs 16:32

Behind the Bathroom Door

Fourteen-year-old Ben Carson sat on the edge of the bathtub and stared at the wall. His heart raced wildly as he realized how close he had come to murdering a neighborhood boy.

The boy had been tormenting him. Flashing his big camping knife, Ben had lunged fiercely at the boy's stomach. His aim was poor; he'd hit the boy's heavy belt buckle instead, breaking the steel blade of his knife.

I might have killed him, Ben thought. *I'm out of control. I've got to do something before I get in real trouble.*

A Word from the Lord

Just then, words from Proverbs came to mind: "He who is slow to anger is better than the mighty, and he who rules his spirit than he who takes a city" (RSV).

Yeah, those words are for me, Ben mused. *If I don't get control, I'll end up in jail, or dead! I guess it's time to ask the Lord for help, like Mother has been telling me to do.*

Ben dropped to his knees on the bathroom floor. "Oh, Lord," he prayed, "take away my temper. I know You can. I believe You will."

Writing about that experience later, Ben said, "The Lord took away my temper, just like that. Whenever I'd feel it begin to boil, it would somehow simmer down as if someone had turned off the burner. I was in awe at what had happened to me."

When Ben grew up, he became a neurosurgeon. The same hand that had almost killed his antagonist when he was fourteen now was used to save lives with his surgeon's scalpel.

His colleagues describe the Ben they know as someone who is unusually calm. Ben knows it wasn't always that way. Before his bathroom conversion, he says, "I would just fly off the handle at the slightest provocation. I would throw rocks and take hammers after people."

What a difference an encounter with God's Word made in Ben's life!

Epilogue

Although he grew up in a single-parent home in the slums of Detroit, Ben won a full scholarship to Yale and graduated from the University of Michigan Medical School. When he was thirty-three years old, Dr. Benjamin Carson became director of pediatric neurosurgery at Johns Hopkins Hospital in Baltimore, Maryland. In 1987, he gained worldwide acclaim for his part in successfully separating Siamese twins joined at the back of the head. He has saved the lives of scores of children who had no other hope of survival.

*For the earth shall be full
of the knowledge of the Lord,
as the waters cover the sea.*

Isaiah 11:9

Now God Speaks Our Language!

"You cowards! Going to war where a million other men will go—and leaving us women to do the Lord's work alone! You are needed in Central America to sell Bibles to people who walk in darkness."

Cameron Townsend was startled by these hard words of blonde, furloughing, single, missionary Stella Zimmerman. While a third-year student at Occidental College in Los Angeles, he had volunteered to go to Guatemala as a Bible salesman. But in 1917, World War I was raging in Europe. The United States was expected to join the war shortly, and Townsend thought it his patriotic duty to forego missionary service and serve his country. But the words of Stella Zimmerman gave him second thoughts.

To Townsend's surprise, the captain of his National

Guard unit agreed to release him, declaring, "You'll do a lot more good selling Bibles in Central America than you would shooting enemy soldiers in France."

Why hasn't God learned our language?

In Guatemala, Townsend was assigned a territory for Bible sales that was largely rural. But the two hundred thousand Cakchiquel Indians who lived there could not read, and they did not understand Spanish. They had no use for the Spanish Bibles he tried to sell them.

"If your God is so smart why hasn't He learned our language?" one of the Cakchiquels asked.

That question startled Cameron again. He thought about this and decided that he would learn their language, reduce it to writing, and translate the Scriptures into Cakchiquel.

With no previous linguistics training, Townsend began this daunting task. He found the Cakchiquel language highly confusing. One verb could be conjugated into a thousand forms, indicating time, location, and many other ideas besides simple action. It was almost impossible.

Then an American archaeologist advised Cameron not to force the language of the Cakchiquels into a Latin mold, but to find the pattern on which that language was based. That counsel revolutionized his method of studying the language. It led him to develop a novel linguistics training program for Bible translators.

When Townsend completed and printed the Gospel

of Mark, the Cakchiquels were delighted. "Now God speaks our language!" they exclaimed.

After spending thirteen years with the Cakchiquels, Townsend decided that God was calling him to do something about the need of hundreds of other tribes that did not have the Scriptures in their own language. He resigned his work in the Central American Mission and founded the Wycliffe Bible Translators and Summer Institute of Linguistics. He did this without the backing of any denomination or any major missionary organization.

For the next fifty years, Cameron Townsend gave his life to making the Bible available to people in their own language.

By 1985, three years after his death, the Wycliffe Bible Translators and Summer School of Linguistics had 6,000 workers working on Bible translations in 1,000 language groups.

The text in father's prayers

What inspired and motivated Cameron Townsend to make such a significant contribution to fulfilling the great commission?

One important influence was that of his father. Cameron himself related how that every weekday morning, before milking the cows, his father read three chapters from the Bible, and five on Sunday. Later after breakfast, he gathered his family for morning devotions. And every day his father ended his prayers with a petition for the fulfillment of Isaiah 11:9. "May the 'knowledge of the Lord' cover the earth 'as the waters cover the sea.' "

Epilogue

The twin organizations that Cameron Townsend founded developed into the largest Protestant missionary organization in the twentieth century. From Latin America, Wycliffe Translators expanded into Africa, Asia, the Pacific Islands, and later into Russia.

In 1963, the Government of Peru awarded Cameron Townsend its Order of Distinguished Service for his help in reducing illiteracy in the country. This was only one of many honors and citations he received through the years. Several American universities offered to confer upon him an honorary doctorate, but he refused them all. He was afraid it would separate him from the simple people he wanted to serve.

In 1966, at his urging, the United States House of Representatives and Senate named September 30 as Bible Translation Day. At a personal meeting with President Nixon in the Oval Office in 1970, Townsend was able to announce, "Mr. President we've just entered our five-hundredth language."

By 1989, Wycliffe Bible Translators had completed over seven hundred translations of the New Testament. Approximately thirty new translations are completed every year. More than one thousand are in the process of translation.

Cameron Townsend founded the first mission in the

history of Christianity that was exclusively dedicated to Bible translation and has been called "the greatest mission strategist of the twentieth century."

Billy Graham called Townsend "the greatest missionary of our time." Ralph Winter, of the U.S. Center for World Missions, named him along with William Carey and Hudson Taylor as "the three most outstanding missionaries of the last two hundred years."

Cameron Townsend would have disagreed. He once said, "The greatest missionary is the Bible in the mother tongue. It never needs a furlough, is never considered a foreigner."

ook unto me, and be ye saved,
all the ends of the earth.

Isaiah 45:22

Finding God in a Snowstorm

Charles was the son of a minister, his mother was a godly woman, but still he did not understand how to find Jesus.

He heard his father preach that all men are destined for the lake of fire and that God in His mercy looks down and picks out a few to be saved. For the rest, there is no hope.

When he was ten years old, Charles came under the conviction of his own sinfulness. He lay awake nights, horrified with the thought that God may not have chosen him for salvation.

He later wrote, "I do not hesitate to say that those who examined my life would not have seen any extraordinary sin, yet as I looked upon myself I saw outrageous sin against God. If I opened my mouth, I spoke amiss. If I sat still there was sin in my silence. I was in custody of the Law. I dared not plunge into grosser vices; I sinned enough without acting like that."

Hoping to find peace with God, Charles visited every church in town during the next four years. He was willing to do anything if only God would forgive him. He heard some terrific sermons about the law and practical Christian living, met several godly men, but not once did he discover the way of salvation.

On the snowy morning of January 6, 1850, fifteen-year-old Charles set out for church. He struggled against the wind and blowing snow. "I can't go any further in this blizzard," Charles told himself. "I've got to get out of this wind."

He turned into a side street to escape the force of the wind. He looked up to see a snow-encrusted sign swaying in the wind. It said, "Artillery Street Primitive Methodist Church." He pushed open the door and went inside.

A dozen people sat in the chapel, bundled up against the cold. Charles took a back seat. The preacher didn't show, so one of the members, a shoemaker, gave the sermon.

What can such a poor, stupid fellow have to say? Charles wondered. *If preachers who have studied in the university aren't able to explain the way of salvation to me, what hope is there to learn from this ignorant fellow?*

Charles cringed as the man began to speak. His grammar was terrible; he couldn't pronounce the words right when he read the text—Isaiah 45:22.

"My dear friends, this is a very simple text indeed," the shoemaker began. "It says, 'Look.' Now that does not take a deal of effort. It ain't lifting your foot or your finger; it is just look. Well, a man need not go to college to learn to look."

There were chuckles in the pews. Even Charles had to smile at the simplicity and truth of what the man said.

"A man need not be worth a thousand a year to look," the laypreacher continued. "Anyone can look; a child can look."

Charles nodded in agreement and wondered what the cobbler would say next.

The man held up the Bible, pointing to the text. "This is what the text says, 'Look unto me.' Aye, many of ye are looking to yourselves. No use looking there. You'll never find comfort in yourselves. Jesus Christ says, 'Look unto me.' "

After about ten minutes of this, the cobbler reached the end of his sermon and made his appeal. He looked at the back row, directly at young Charles, and shouted, "Young man, you look very miserable!"

Charles blinked. He wasn't used to having preachers in the pulpit make remarks on his personal appearance.

The lay preacher went on, "And you will always be miserable if you do not obey my text. But if you obey now, you will be saved. Young man, look to Jesus Christ and be saved! Look! Look! Look!"

Charles did look to Jesus that night, and the burden of his guilt rolled away. He walked home that day hardly noticing the cold, for he had been warmed with the good news of the gospel. He was so filled with joy that he felt like singing and shouting his praise to everyone he met.

The following May, Charles Haddon Spurgeon walked eight miles to be baptized in the River Lark near his home. He had already decided to enter the ministry. He determined that every sermon he preached would make the way of salvation as clear as that poor shoe-maker had done that snowy night.

Epilogue

Charles Spurgeon became the pastor of a Baptist church in Waterbeach, England, when he was sixteen. The twelve members grew to over one hundred in two years.

By the age of twenty-two, he was declared "the most popular preacher of his day."

On March 25, 1861, at the age of 26, he preached his first sermon in the London Metropolitan Tabernacle, where he later often preached to an audience of ten thousand people. On one occasion, 23,654 people showed up. It is even reported that Queen Victoria went once in disguise to hear him preach. He baptized more than fourteen thousand people in his lifetime.

Spurgeon preached twelve to thirteen times a week.

More than two thousand of his sermons were published. His sermons sold an average of twenty-five thousand copies each. One sermon sold 230,000 copies.

He founded a pastors' college and an orphanage for 500 children. He established a Bible society that employed ninety colporteurs. He published a monthly magazine.

Spurgeon died in 1892. However, his sermons were published weekly until 1917. As one commentator put it, "He was the most popular and the greatest preacher of his age."

*A*ll we like sheep have gone astray;
 we have turned every one to his own way;
 and the Lord hath laid on him the iniquity of us all.
Isaiah 53:6

The Unanswered Question

Solomon Ginsberg walked the streets of London feeling alone and forsaken. At fourteen, he had left home in protest when his father arranged for his marriage to the twelve-year-old daughter of a wealthy merchant. Now, he wondered if he had been too hasty. Just a few days before, he had arrived in London with three nickels in his pocket hoping to find work so that he could earn his passage on a ship to the United States.

He was walking down Whitechapel Road in the Jewish section of London's East End, when a man called, "Come hear God's message for Jews!"

Guess I might as well, Solomon thought. *I've nothing better to do right now. Maybe God will tell me what to do.*

The Unanswered Question

A man stood up, opened his Bible, and began to read Isaiah 53. Solomon found his breath coming a little quicker. He leaned forward, the words taking him back to the time he had read those same words in his father's house in Poland.

How well he remembered that autumn. Ever since Solomon could remember, his father had built a special hut near the house each fall. It's roof was covered with branches and was called a sukkah.

"It is to remind us of the many years our Jewish ancestors spent living in the wilderness after our deliverance from Egypt," Father had explained each year.

The year he turned thirteen, Father had invited him into the booth, where several adults had gathered for the nine-day celebration of the Feast of Tabernacles. Bored with their talk, Solomon reached for a book lying on the table. It fell open to Isaiah 53. He read, "He was wounded for our transgressions. . . . All we like sheep have gone astray; we have turned every one to his own way, and the Lord hath laid on him the iniquity of us all."

"Who is Isaiah writing about in chapter 53?" Solomon blurted out. Father looked startled but said nothing.

"Well, who is it?" Solomon insisted.

Mr. Ginsberg grabbed the book from Solomon's hands and slapped the boy across the face.

I still wonder who Isaiah was writing about, Solomon thought, focusing his eyes on the speaker. He soon learned that the man of Isaiah 53 was the Messiah, Jesus Christ. He learned that Jesus died on Calvary's cross for everyone in the world, even for him, Solomon Ginsberg. Solomon decided to accept the Messiah as his Saviour.

Epilogue

Solomon soon found a job, but when his employer learned of his decision, he was fired. He wandered the streets until taken into a home for Jewish Christians. An uncle came from Poland to persuade him to give up his faith. Solomon refused and was disinherited. He never heard from his family again. For thirty-three years, he served as a missionary in Brazil.

Then shall ye call upon me,
and ye shall go and pray unto me,
and I will hearken unto you.
And ye shall seek me, and find me,
when ye shall search for me with all your heart.

Jeremiah 29:12, 13

It's This Week or Never!

It was Sunday night, October 7, 1821. Twenty-nine-year-old law student Charles Finney tossed in his bed, thinking about the condition of his soul.

I must make my peace with God, Charles decided at last. *It is this week or never. It doesn't matter how much work there is to do in the office; I am going to lay everything else aside and give my attention to the salvation of my soul.* That settled, Charles Finney went to sleep.

Finney had arrived in Adams, New York in 1818 to begin his studies, ignorant of the Bible and Christianity. However, he noticed that several law scholars referred to the laws of Moses, so he purchased a Bible and kept it on his desk in the law office. He read it from time to time, but found it hard to understand. Charles attended church regularly and often argued with the minister but could come to no clear understanding of how to be saved.

On Monday morning, true to his decision, Charles went to his office determined to find God. He locked the door and plugged the keyhole. *I don't want anyone to know I'm praying*, he thought.

He sat down at his desk and took out the Bible and read for a bit. Someone knocked at the door. "Just a minute!" Charles called, quickly shoving the Bible under some open law books. He didn't want anyone to know what he was doing.

At the end of the day, Charles still had not discovered how to find God. He was ashamed to talk to anyone, lest they discover what a terrible sinner he was and how ignorant of how to find peace with God. Tuesday was no better. He could not pray. He could not repent. He could not find God.

Tuesday night, Charles lay awake most of the night, afraid to go to sleep for fear he would die without making his peace with God. A terrible heaviness settled on his mind, and once again he spent the night tossing and turning.

Wednesday morning, on the way to the office, Charles heard a voice speaking to his heart, "What are you waiting for, Charles? Didn't you promise to give your heart to God?"

"Yes! Yes!" Charles mumbled. "I will do it this very

day or die in the trying!"

Instead of going to his office, Charles made for a grove of trees north of the village. He sneaked along a stone wall, dodging behind bushes and doing all he could to make sure no one knew where he was nor where he was going.

Once inside the woods, he kept going another quarter mile until he came to a nook that was enclosed by fallen trees. There, he got on his knees and began to pray. Something rustled the leaves. Charles opened his eyes, expecting to see that someone had followed him. He saw nothing but a squirrel looking for acorns.

"You should be ashamed of yourself, Finney!" Charles said, shaking his head. "How wicked you are that you are even afraid that someone will see you on your knees before God!" Tears blurred his vision, and he felt he would choke.

He cried out then, "I will not leave this place if all the men on earth and all the devils in hell surround me!"

At that very moment, a verse popped into his mind. He couldn't remember ever reading it before but knew at once that it was the Word of God. The words were, "Then . . . ye shall go and pray unto me, and I will hearken unto you. And ye shall seek me, and find me, when ye shall search for me with all your heart."

"Lord, I take You at Your Word!" Charles cried. "Now You know I am searching for You with all my heart. That's why I've come here to the woods to pray. You have promised to hear me. I know You don't lie, and therefore I will find You!"

Sudden joy flooded Charles's being. Promise after promise of Scripture began pouring into his mind. And with each verse, Charles said, "Yes, Lord. I accept that as Your Word. I'm going to hold on to that one."

After some time, Charles stood and headed back for the village. He had left for the woods just after breakfast, and it was now time for dinner. *I have been in that woods for hours!* Charles realized. *But so happy was I that it seemed but a moment.* He tried to think of his sins but could remember none of them. He felt a sense of God's presence and an assurance that his sins were all forgiven.

That afternoon, he worked with others to move their office furnishings to a new location. After the others were gone, Charles put his books in order, then built a fire and sat down to think. Feeling the urge to pray, he went to an adjoining room and shut the door. About this experience he wrote, "There was no fire, and no light . . . nevertheless it appeared to me as if it were perfectly light . . . It seemed as if I met the Lord Jesus Christ face to face . . . It seemed to me that I saw him as I would see any other man. He said nothing, but looked at me in such a manner as to break me right down at his feet."

Charles knelt there for a long time, overjoyed at last that He had found the One for whom he had been searching. He wept and prayed for a long while, and when he returned to his study, the fire had nearly burned to ashes.

Epilogue

Charles Grandison Finney gave up his study of law and became a preacher. Under his leadership, numerous revivals broke out in New York and New England from 1821 to 1832.

Finney later settled down to pastor churches in New York, then in Oberlin, Ohio, where he was president of Oberlin College for fifteen years. He wrote several books; one of them, *Lectures on Revival*, was a manual for the Finney method of planning for revival.

*W*here is he that is born King of the Jews?
for we have seen his star in the east,
and are come to worship him.

Matthew 2:2

The Greatest Since Paul

"I don't believe in God anymore, so I see no reason why I shouldn't live the way I want. I've quit teaching and I'm going to New York to make a name for myself," twenty-year-old Adoniram Judson announced to his parents.

"Just what do you intend to do with your life?" his father, a respected minister, wanted to know.

"I intend to be a great man," Adoniram proclaimed. "Maybe I'll be an orator, a poet, a lawyer, a statesman, or perhaps a play-writer." Adoniram turned away when he saw the pain on his father's face, the tears in his mother's eyes.

"We'll be praying for you, son," Pastor Judson said.

In New York, Adoniram joined a theatrical group but

soon left that to try something else. Wandering about the country, he happened to stay overnight in a country inn. The owner mentioned to him that there was a man sick in the room next to him who would probably die during the night. "I hope this won't disturb you," he said. "The walls are quite thick."

"I don't expect it will," Adoniram replied. "I'm tired enough after my journey to sleep through almost anything!"

However, that night Adoniram tossed and turned on his bed. *I wonder if he is a Christian? I wonder if he has hope of a hereafter? Or is he a deist like me, having Christian parents who weep and pray for him every day?*

The next morning at breakfast, Adoniram asked the proprietor, "How's the gentleman that was sick?"

"He's gone, poor fellow," the man replied. "Dead."

"Who was he?" Adoniram asked.

"A young man from Providence College, a very fine fellow," he replied.

"Really? Providence College? That is my alma mater. Could you tell me his name?"

"Eames, Jacob Eames. Did you know him?"

"Know him?" Adoniram was shocked. "He was my best friend all through college!" The truth was that Jacob Eames was the very one who had convinced Adoniram to give up Christianity to become a deist. Suddenly, Adoniram realized that the future for Eames and for himself was without hope.

Going back to his room, he packed and left immediately for home. There he enrolled in Andover Theological College to study the Bible and see if he could find God. In May of 1809, near the close of the first school year, Adoniram accepted Christ as his Saviour and joined the church.

Four months later, in September, Adoniram read a sermon by Pastor Buchanan based on Matthew 2:2. The pamphlet was an appeal for people to go as missionaries to foreign lands where many, like the wise men, were seeking God that they might worship Him.

Over and over Adoniram read the sermon and the story of the wise men in Matthew 2. *Could it be that God is calling me to be a missionary for Him in some faraway land?* Adoniram wondered. *What a thrill it would be to take the gospel to people who are worshiping gods of wood and stone, seeking for peace and salvation, but never finding it because there was no one to tell them about the true God.*

Adoniram could think of nothing else except that sermon and that text. He skipped his classes to pray and study. For several days, he did no other study, but he focused on Matthew 2:2, wondering if God was really calling him to go. The thought excited, yet frightened, him, and he could come to no conclusion.

Adoniram went back to classes but thought often about the call he felt to mission service. He struggled with the idea in prayer and on long walks in the woods. In February 1810, after six months of thinking about mission service, he took another walk alone in the woods to pray and meditate upon Matthew 2:2.

"Lord, I'm feeling half inclined to give it up," Adoniram prayed at last. "I can come to no decision, so I think I'll just forget about it."

Suddenly into his mind came the words of Christ, "Go ye into all the world, and preach the gospel to every creature." The words were so clear, so powerful, that Adoniram knew it was the Holy Spirit speaking directly to him.

"All right, Lord," Adoniram said. "I will do it. I will accept your call to mission service. Though great difficulties appear in my way, I am resolved to obey your command at all events!"

Two years later, he and his wife sailed from Boston harbor for India—America's first foreign missionaries. Like the "Star in the East," Adoniram Judson led many to worship the Saviour.

Epilogue

Although sent out by the Congregational churches in New England, the Judsons studied the Bible with Baptist missionaries en route and were baptized by immersion upon arrival in India. Hearing of this, the Baptists in the United States formed a missionary organization and took up his support.

After a brief survey of the situation in Calcutta, where the East India Company discouraged mission work, the Judsons sailed for Rangoon, Burma (Myanmar).

Adoniram worked in Burma for thirty-seven years, learning to speak Burmese fluently. During this time, the English and Burmese were at war, and Adoniram spent many months in prison under dreadful conditions. When he died, he left behind a translation of the Bible into Burmese and a Burmese-English dictionary.

He was "the greatest of all American missionaries," according to Dr. George Smith. He writes: "Adoniram Judson is surpassed by no missionary since the apostle Paul in devotion and scholarship, in labors and perils, in saintliness and humility, in the result of his toils."

*B*lessed are the poor in spirit:
for their's is the kingdom of heaven. . . .
Blessed are the merciful: for they shall obtain mercy.
Blessed are the pure in heart: for they shall see God. . . .
Blessed are ye, when men shall revile you.
Matthew 5:3-11

Chance Meeting
on a Train

Narayan Tilak was born in the Ratnagiri area of Maharastra, India. His parents were Chitpawan Brahmins, the highest caste of Hindus in western India.

Tilak was deeply prejudiced against Christianity from childhood. He claimed to be the sworn enemy of Christ and His followers. He had never met a Christian preacher nor read a single page of the Bible, but he had heard many things against the Christian faith.

Then one day, he was invited by the king of the small state of Rajnandgaon in India to be a teacher and government clerk. He got on the train at Nagpur to go to Rajnandgaon. As he entered the train, he saw a European sitting in the compartment.

Oh! Oh! I'm in trouble! Tilak thought. *This is British*

India. The Sahibs don't allow Indians to sit with them in the train. Even though I'm a high caste Brahmin, I'll be disgraced.

He relaxed when the European flashed a smile of welcome and moved over to make a place for him. *This European has some manners*, he thought. *He may not be so bad after all.*

As the train gathered speed, they fell into friendly conversation. When the European heard that Tilak was a teacher, he asked his opinion about a Sanskrit poem and its writer.

Tilak was surprised again. *How could this Sahib be interested in our poetry? He really is different! I kind of like him.*

Their conversation turned from poetry to philosophy, then to spiritual things. Quietly the Sahib asked, "What do you think of Jesus Christ and his teachings?"

Tilak replied honestly, "I really don't know what Jesus taught."

The Sahib shared a few of the sayings of Jesus such as, "Love your enemies. Do good to those who hate you." That sounded interesting.

After a long conversation, the European said, "God is drawing you, young man. Study the Bible. Apply yourself wholeheartedly to the life of Christ, and you will become a Christian."

That's a rather rash speech, Tilak thought. *I will never become a Christian!*

After saying a prayer, Tilak's new friend pulled a copy

of the New Testament from his luggage and offered it to Tilak as a gift. Wanting to be polite, Tilak promised to read it, even though he disliked the book as soon as he saw it.

When he reached Rajnandgaon, Tilak decided to keep his promise and read the New Testament from beginning to end. However, he only got as far as Matthew 5 and the Sermon on the Mount.

He was captivated by the beauty and the great philosophical depth of sayings such as, "Blessed are the pure in heart: for they shall see God." He found the jewel-like sentences filled with love, mercy, and truth. "Blessed are the merciful: for they shall obtain mercy." He found the answer to the most difficult questions of Hindu philosophy in those chapters. Problems such as that of rebirth were fully resolved. "Blessed are the poor in spirit: for their's is the kingdom of heaven."

Tilak was astonished! He was filled with a longing to know Christ's teaching more and more. He read the New Testament through to Revelation. And he saw his prayers answered by Christ, one after another. He was totally amazed.

When his family discovered Tilak's interest in Christianity, they totally disowned and disinherited him. Narayan found the Lord was very close to him in the troubles that he endured. His wife left him, and through that, he lost his child. He then lost his job. He experienced severe opposition and reproach, but he felt God with him each hour!

Although he was a Brahmin and of the social group from which priests are selected, he lost all caste when he became a Christian. To the Hindu, losing caste is the greatest of all disasters. He had now become as a low caste person, and anyone from his family would be defiled if they had anything to do with him.

Tilak decided to let the world know that he was a Christian. He published his testimony in an Indian Christian periodical. This caused a widespread stir in India. He was baptized in Bombay in the American Mission Church within two years of receiving the New Testament on the train.

About his conversion Tilak wrote, "Could anyone have conceived that this man, so proud of the Hindu religion, would propose to forsake it and glory in the Bible, abandoning himself to the will of God?

"Nevertheless this, my pride perished, and today I stand like a small child before God holding the hand of Christ. Is it any wonder that people should see this and be astonished? I myself am astonished. I had no intention of becoming a Christian."

Epilogue

Narayan Tilak used his gifts as a poet to write hundreds of Christian hymns (bhajans) in the Marathi language. They are widely used among Indian Christians today. He also translated many English hymns into Marathi.

Later, Tilak's wife returned to him, and she also became a Christian, having suffered severe persecution from her family.

He published his story in the book *I Follow After* through the Oxford University Press in England. He was later ordained in the Presbyterian Mission of Maharasta.

Tilak began writing the life of Christ in verse form, the Christayan, but was unable to complete it before his death in 1919.

lessed are they that mourn:
for they shall be comforted.

Matthew 5:4

A Scrap of Paper

Haymin Herschell walked the streets of Paris in a daze. He wandered through its parks and along the banks of the River Seine, oblivious to the traffic around him. He had just learned of his mother's death in Strzelno, Poland. Haymin's grief seemed more than he could bear.

"She's gone! She's gone!" Over and over he told himself the awful truth. "Haymin, your loving mother is no more!"

He wished he hadn't left home at fifteen to study at Berlin University. He wished he hadn't been so restless, traveling from Berlin, to London, and back to Paris. He wished he could see his mother once more, that things were as they had been when he was a child.

He thought of his childhood, how his mother and father had gathered him each day for prayers. He remembered his mother's careful preparation for each Sabbath, the special food, the candles, and the blessing.

He remembered the feast days, especially the day of atonement. He remembered seeing his mother weep as she said, "We have now no temple, no high priest, no altar, and no sacrifices."

And now he had no mother, and it seemed to Haymin that even God had forsaken him. He felt burdened down with sorrow for his mother's death and for his own miserable condition. He struggled to find peace but could not. He felt that his sins had separated him from God and there was no hope.

"O God, I have no one to help me," Haymin cried out in his despair. It was the first time he had ever prayed a prayer from his own heart. Always before, he had recited written prayers that he had learned in childhood. Now he cast these aside, needing to express the real feelings of his soul.

"I dare not approach Thee, for I am guilty," Haymin prayed. "O help me, for the sake of my father Abraham who was willing to offer up his son Isaac. Have mercy upon me and impute his righteousness unto me."

The echo of his prayer died away, and there was no answering blessing from God. He felt no peace, no comfort, no hope. "Oh, God, have you cast me off forever?" he cried. "Have you forsaken me?"

A few days later, while unwrapping something he had bought in the market, by chance he noticed the words "Blessed are they that mourn: for they shall be comforted."

Smoothing out the paper, he read more. The words

were beautiful, filling him with a sense of peace and hope. *I wonder who wrote those words?* Haymin thought. He turned the paper over, but there was no indication of the author or the source. *I would certainly like to find the book this came from!*

Not long after that, Haymin was visiting in the home of a Christian friend, where he noticed a copy of the New Testament. Curious, he picked it up and thumbed through its pages, reading a little here and there. Then he saw the same words he had found on the scrap of paper from the market, "Blessed are they that mourn: for they shall be comforted."

So that's where those words came from, the New Testament, Haymin mused. *I wonder if all of it is like this.*

"May I borrow this book for a while?" Haymin asked his friend. "It looks interesting."

"No problem," his friend agreed. "Keep it as long as you like."

Once back in his room, Haymin began to read the New Testament in earnest. About the experience, he wrote, "I was so shocked by the constant recurrence of the name of Jesus that I cast the book aside. At length, I determined to read it through."

It was a good story. Haymin felt compassion for Jesus and hatred for His murderers. Gradually, as he continued to read, the truth dawned upon him that Jesus Christ had died for the sins of Haymin Herschell. As he studied, he was convinced that the Old Testament and the New Testament were equally the Word of God.

"Lord, I believe Jesus is the Messiah," Haymin prayed. "He is the Redeemer and King of Israel, who was wounded for our transgressions and bruised for our iniquities. For His sake have mercy upon me and give me peace."

From that day forth, Haymin Herschell had peace.

Epilogue

When Haymin was baptized, he took the name of Pastor Henry C. Ridley, a Christian he admired greatly. After that, he was known as Ridley H. Herschell and became a minister, working for other Jews.

Herschell led five of his brothers to Christ, and three of them became ministers. In 1842, he helped found the British Society for the Propagation of the Gospel Among the Jews. This developed into the Society for Distributing the Scriptures to the Jews, with which Herschell worked until his death in 1864. Five hundred policemen were in the procession that followed Herschell's coffin to the cemetery. They had been members of his weekly Bible class.

Herschell was the author of several books designed to promote the gospel among the Jews. He edited a magazine called *The Voice of Israel*.

His son, Lord Farrer Herschell, became a lawyer and was elected as Member of Parliament for the City of Durham. He served as Solicitor General under Gladstone, and later became Lord Chancellor. He served on a commission to settle the border between Canada and Alaska. He was also a devoted Christian like his father.

Therefore whosoever heareth
these sayings of mine,
and doeth them, I will liken him unto a wise man,
which built his house upon a rock.
Matthew 7:24

God Speaks in Hollywood

In spite of the importance of the bride and groom, the minister was two hours late to the wedding because of a snowstorm. Before the ceremony, there was a fire in the Oklahoma ranch house where the wedding was held. Shortly after the wedding, the storm turned into a blizzard that closed the whole area for two days.

That New Year's Eve, 1947, movie star, entertainer, and King of the Cowboys, Roy Rogers, married his leading lady, Dale Evans—Queen of the West.

The wedding day difficulties were a harbinger of more problems to come. Dale's acting career came to a screeching halt shortly afterward. The movie studio told Roy that he had to have a new leading lady. They said that the kids who watched the movies wouldn't believe the stories on the screen if they knew that Roy and his costar were married in real life. The romantic mystique of their relationship was gone. Dale's loss of identity as a star caused her serious emotional stress.

The death of Roy's previous wife had left him a widower with three small children. These three were not about to accept his new wife as their stepmother. One day as Dale was moving the furniture in the living room, the five-year-old girl objected. "That's not your furniture. It's my mommy's!"

Dale was in a serious crisis, and she knew it. Then her twenty-year-old son, Tom, came for a visit. Tom was an active Christian. "You need the Lord's help to get you through your problems," he suggested. "You should start taking the family to church. You will find that God will help you through all the difficulties you are facing."

That Sunday evening, she attended church with Tom. Dr. Jack MacArthur preached on Matthew 7:24: "Therefore whosoever heareth these sayings of mine, and doeth them, I will liken him unto a wise man, which built his house upon a rock."

Pastor MacArthur asserted, "Anyone who builds his or her life on faith in Jesus Christ will succeed against anything that comes, be it sickness, death, financial reverses, selfishness, or lies."

This message is aimed at me, Dale thought. *God is speaking to me! I should go up to the altar tonight, but what would people say? What will they think if I pub-*

licly admit that I'm a sinner. The gossip columnists would love it. It would be all over Hollywood within twenty-four hours.

"Why don't you go?" Tom whispered. "Why not make it right with the Lord now? Give Him your life, and let Him give you the peace you need?"

"I'm already a Christian," she replied defensively.

"You don't know Christ," Tom shook his head. "You've been into all that Eastern philosophy stuff, and it hasn't given you peace. You need to know Christ, and He will give you peace."

"Give me until next week," Dale answered. "I need time to think." The truth was she just didn't have the courage to go down that aisle, although she desperately wanted to.

Tom turned away, his eyes filled with tears.

All the way home, Dale's mind was in a turmoil of conflicting emotions. She didn't know what to do. Roy was away on a trip, and she couldn't talk to him when she got home. She went to her bedroom alone and fell on her knees, sobbing out her prayer to God. She remembered that when she was ten years old, she had accepted Jesus as her Saviour, kind of like fire insurance, but she had never accepted Him as her Lord.

There on her knees that night, Dale made her surrender. She prayed, "Lord, if You will forgive me and let me live until next Sunday, I will go down that aisle and make a public confession!"

The next Sunday, she practically bounced down the

aisle when the appeal was made. An indescribable peace washed into her heart, cleansing and purifying her soul. She got up feeling that a crushing burden had fallen from her back. She felt like she was walking on clouds. The sky looked brighter, the grass seemed greener, and the flowers had more beautiful colors than she had ever seen.

When she came home from church, she was changed so much that her husband, Roy, noticed it. "What's happened to you?" he asked.

"I've done the most wonderful thing I've ever done in my life!" Dale exclaimed. "I've given my life to Jesus Christ to follow Him."

"Well, don't start working on me," Roy said. "You can leave me out of it."

Several weeks later, they had a Hollywood party in their home. Roy became angry with Dale for some comments she made when one of his leading ladies asked why she didn't serve alcohol.

However, the next day, Roy went to church with Dale and accepted Christ for himself.

Epilogue

Dale Evans Rogers and her husband Roy are two of the best-known Christian believers in the Hollywood entertainment industry. She is the mother of nine children, a singer, actress, speaker, and the author of twenty-five books.

She was named Texan of the Year by the Texas Press

Association and Church Woman of the Year in 1967. In 1989, she was named Grandmother of the Year.

Her book *Angel Unaware* about her child with Down's Syndrome is regarded as a classic. Her chosen area of service has been in charities that help abused and retarded children.

The story of Dale Evans Rogers's growing Christian experience is told in her book *In the Hands of the Potter*. "I am convinced that God is reaching out to us, allowing experiences that will help us develop into the kind of people He can use," she writes.

*I was hungry and you gave Me food;
I was thirsty and you gave Me drink;
I was a stranger and you took Me in;
I was naked and you clothed Me;
I was sick and you visited Me (NKJV).*

Matthew 25:35, 36

The Unexpected Guest

It was Saturday morning. Margaret Brand watched the cycle rickshaw pull up to her bungalow on the campus of Vellore Medical College. *I wonder who that could be?* she mused.

She went out to meet a slim, young man, stepping out of the rickshaw. She noticed the white scars on his face, his heavily bandaged feet, the way he shielded his eyes from the glare of the sun. *He's a leper!* Margaret decided.

"Hello!" she greeted him. "How may I help you?"

"I've come to see Dr. Paul Brand," he said.

"Oh, I'm so sorry," Margaret replied. "Dr. Brand is out of town. He'll not be back until Tuesday." The man nodded sadly and turned to leave.

Margaret watched as he hobbled down the road. *Poor*

man, I hope he has somewhere to go. He looks so disappointed.

A Change of Heart

In that moment, the words she had read for her morning devotions pierced her thoughts: "I was a stranger and you took Me in." She called after him, "Wait! Please come back!"

"Do you have a place to stay in town?" she asked.

He shook his head. Slowly, she coaxed him to tell his story. Diagnosed with leprosy at the age of eight, he had become a social outcast, rejected by friends, shunned by the community, ignored and despised. He had finally graduated from a mission school, but no one would hire him. Then someone told him about Dr. Brand. He had used the last money he possessed to hire the rickshaw. He had no money, no friends, and no idea where to go.

"Come stay with us," Margaret invited. "We'd be honored to have you as our guest!"

When Paul returned on Tuesday, he was upset. "How could you do it, Margaret?" he exclaimed. "You have put our children at risk!"

"But, Paul, he had nowhere to go!" she replied. Then she told him of the text she had read Saturday morning. "How could I not take him in?" she asked.

Epilogue

About this incident, Dr. Brand later wrote that it was a decision for which he would be eternally grateful. He said, "Besides teaching us about our own exaggerated fears, Sadan became one of our dearest friends."

Dr. and Mrs. Paul Brand worked at Vellore Medical College in India for twenty years, establishing leprosy rehabilitation facilities at Karigiri. They later served in the U.S. Public Health Service leprosarium in Carville, Louisiana.

Whosoever will save his life shall lose it;
but whosoever shall lose his life for my sake
and the gospel's, the same shall save it.

Mark 8:35

The Price of Happiness

Twenty-one-year-old Albert Schweitzer awoke to the sound of birds singing in the orchards around his home in Gunsbach, Germany. Brilliant sunlight streamed through his open window.

Ah! What a day to be alive! Albert thought. He looked out his window past the steeple of the village church to the lush countryside. *Why am I so blessed, while others live such lives of misery? What is the price of such happiness? Surely I can't just take my good fortune for granted.*

For some time, Albert had been struggling with similar thoughts. It seemed incomprehensible to him that he should be allowed to lead such a happy life, while he saw so many people around him wrestling with care and suffering.

Albert closed his eyes and recalled the verse that had been his meditation for several months. He had been trying to figure out what it meant to him personally, that strange verse in Mark 8:35, "Whosoever shall lose his life for my sake . . . shall save it."

Suddenly, the meaning flashed into his mind with the brilliance of the morning sun. *I must give myself in direct service of humanity, not talking or preaching, but simply doing, showing Christ's love by helping to relieve the misery of others.*

Albert's heart beat a little faster as he made a solemn vow, *I will consider myself justified in living till I am thirty for science and art. I will then give myself entirely to the service of humanity.* About this decision he later wrote, "Now the answer was found. In addition to the outward, I now had inward happiness."

Nine years later, on October 13, 1905, Albert walked briskly down the Avenue de la Grande Armee in Paris and dropped several letters into the post box. One was resigning his post as principal of the Theological College of St. Thomas. Others were sent to his parents and friends informing them that at the beginning of the winter term he would enroll as a medical student to prepare himself to go to Africa as a doctor.

Epilogue

By the age of 30, Albert Schweitzer was well known as a theologian, organist, authority on organ building, and an interpreter of the music of Johann Sebastian Bach. He studied medicine from 1905 to 1913, then went as a missionary doctor to Labarene, French Equatorial Africa (now Gabon). A chicken coop served as his first consulting room for his jungle hospital.

In 1928, Schweitzer received the Goethe prize and in 1952, the Nobel Peace Prize. He used the $33,000 prize money to expand his hospital and set up a leper colony. In 1955, Queen Elizabeth II conferred on him Great Britain's highest civilian award, the Order of Merit.

*What shall it profit a man,
if he shall gain the whole world,
and lose his own soul?
Or what shall a man give in exchange for his soul?*
Mark 8:36, 37

Street Corner Invitation

It was the evening of January 3, 1814. A cold sleet had just fallen. Now the air was frosty and the ground slippery as eighteen-year-old John Williams made his way to a certain street corner on City Road. There he had planned to meet some friends who had promised to spend the evening with him at a nearby tavern.

John, hands stuffed in his pockets to keep warm, paced the street, anxiously looking for his companions. They were nowhere in sight.

The evening chimes were playing from the church tower, and scores of people hastened along the slippery road toward the sound. One of these was Mrs. Tonkin, wife of the local ironmonger. As she passed John, she looked twice. *Who is that young man?* she wondered.

He looks so familiar. Oh yes. Of course. It is my husband's apprentice. I've seen him in the workshop.

Turning around, Mrs. Tonkin approached the tall, young man. "John, what are you doing here?"

"I was supposed to meet some friends to go to the tavern, but they haven't showed," he admitted. "I sure wish they'd come, because it's cold out tonight."

"Forget the tavern," Mrs. Tonkin advised. "Come along with me to Moorfields Tabernacle."

"That's OK," he replied. Church was the last place he wanted to go just then.

"Oh, come on, John," she urged pleasantly. "At least come for a little while to warm up. I think you'll enjoy Pastor East."

Reluctantly, John agreed, walking with Mrs. Tonkin to the church not far away. The warmth felt good. He settled in a back seat to listen for a few moments to the sermon.

"What shall it profit a man if he gain the whole world and lose his own soul," Pastor East was saying. The impact on John was powerful. *He's talking about me!* John realized. *I've been seeking the world and it's pleasures but am losing out on eternity.* John stayed for the whole service and accepted Christ as his Saviour that night.

Epilogue

Two years later, John Williams went as a missionary to the South Sea Islands, settling first in Raiatea, one of the Society Islands. On Raratonga, John built *The Messenger of Peace*, the first of five missionary boats he built to take the gospel to outlying islands. He had to make his own forge, fasten boards with wooden pegs, made rope of bark, and sails of woven mats. He visited every significant island within a two thousand mile radius. He was martyred on Erromanga on November 20, 1839. His death inspired new enthusiasm for missions.

Thou art not far from the kingdom of God.
Mark 12:34

Not Far From the Kingdom

John Wesley sailed from England bound for Savannah, Georgia. His goal was to convert the Native American Indians. On board ship, crossing the Atlantic, there was a terrible storm, and Wesley feared for his life. However, he noticed that the Moravian Christians on board did not seem to be afraid, though the waves literally swept over the place where they were meeting for worship. Watching them, John Wesley realized that though he was deeply religious, he lacked genuine saving faith.

Wesley's mission to Georgia was a failure, and he fled back to England. He felt that though he had gone to convert the Indians, he himself had never been truly converted.

One day he counseled with Peter Boehler, the leader

of a Moravian group in London. "Should I resign from the ministry until I have saving faith?" Wesley wanted to know.

"No," Peter advised him. "Preach faith until you have faith and then preach it because you have it!"

Wesley resolved to find true saving faith and a genuine conversion experience. He continued his search until May 24, 1738. That morning, before going out, he was leafing through his Bible and suddenly discovered Jesus' words in Mark 12:34, "Thou art not far from the kingdom of God."

Perhaps there's hope that I'll soon find saving faith, Wesley thought. That evening, he went to a Moravian Society meeting at Aldersgate. A layleader read Luther's preface to the Book of Romans. At about a quarter to nine, Wesley felt his heart strangely warmed.

I do have faith! Wesley realized. *I do trust Christ, and I have been saved from the law of sin and death.* Joy filled his heart! He knew that he had entered the kingdom at last!

Epilogue

Wesley's conversion is widely recognized as a significant event in Christian history, for it marks the beginning of Methodism, which has had a great impact on Britain, the United States, and the world. Within a year of the Aldersgate experience, Wesley started preaching outdoors. Crowds of ten and twenty thousand listened to him.

For the next fifty years, he traveled sixty or seventy miles a day on horseback, preached several times daily, beginning at five in the morning. His work initiated a tremendous revival of personal religious experience for multitudes.

He traveled a total of 250,000 miles on the roads of England, Scotland, and Ireland; preached 42,000 sermons, and published 233 books! Through his tireless and incessant labor, the face of British society was changed and its religion altered forever.

The leaders he selected and the system he organized enabled the Methodist Church to become a major Protestant denomination, with a worldwide membership of over 40 million.

*H*e arose, and came to his father.
But when he was yet a great way off,
his father saw him, and had compassion, and ran,
and fell on his neck, and kissed him.

Luke 15:20

*A*mazing *G*race

John Newton, author of the much loved hymn "Amazing Grace," first went to sea on his father's vessel when he was eleven years old. At sea, he ran with the rough of the crew and learned their coarse and blasphemous speech.

His godly mother had prayed with him every day and sought to fill his heart with Scripture from his early childhood. But she died when he was only six, and he was left in the care of servants while his father was at sea. In his early days before the mast, he tried to forget his mother's prayers and discovered he could get a hearty laugh from his fellows by twisting the words of Scripture into irreverent jokes.

His father got him good appointments on vessels with

his friends, but Newton was irresponsible and untrust-worthy, ending up as the lowest of the crew.

One day, he was forced by a press gang to serve on a naval vessel. There, his back was lashed raw for dis-obeying orders. Later, on the coast of Africa, while serv-ing a slave-trader, he was subjected to the meanest of treatment at the hand of that man's slaves.

On the return voyage to England, a terrible storm threatened to sink the vessel on which he was sailing. The fearful captain wanted to throw him overboard, worried that he was a Jonah running from God, bring-ing disaster to all. But with great effort, Newton helped them save the ship, finally lashing himself to the wheel for eleven hours until the storm was gone.

During those frantic hours, Newton's conscience was aroused and the words of Scripture taught by his pray-ing mother came back to mind. He, too, thought with the crew that God was punishing him for his infidelity. He felt that his sins were too great to be forgiven. But when the ship did not sink and the storm began to abate, he thought he saw the hand of God showing favor, and he began to pray.

Their troubles were far from over. Their provisions were almost entirely lost, and since they had stuffed their thick clothes into the holes and nailed them with boards during the storm, they now faced the cold without proper cloth-ing. Further, the ship had lost most of its sails, and there was no hope that they would meet another vessel.

Newton spent those days praying and reading the

Bible, hoping to find his way back to God. He longed to find forgiveness for his sins. The passage that struck his mind with power was the story of the prodigal son in Luke 15:11-32. He saw himself in that story and realized that Jesus had told the story to give him hope. He believed in the mercy of God. From that day on, John Newton was a new man, born again through the grace of God. He was twenty-three years old.

Epilogue

Seven years later, Newton gave up his life as a master of vessels at sea and became the surveyor of tides for the Port of Liverpool. Within a few months, the Great Earthquake struck Lisbon, November 1, 1775, killing 60,000 people.

How easily I could have been in Lisbon! Newton thought. It was then he realized that he had done nothing to prepare others to meet God. He took up preaching, sharing his own conversion experience as an example of what God's grace can do for others. He came under conviction that he should enter the ministry. He studied Greek and Hebrew privately in preparation for his profession.

When he applied for a pastorate, both the bishop of Chester and the Archbishop of York refused him. The enduring popularity of Newton's hymns reveals the lack of foresight by the Archbishop of York who refused to ordain him because he had no formal theological education.

The Earl of Dartmouth providentially read the first draft of Newton's book about his seafaring and conversion experiences, and appointed him his minister at Olney. Newton was then thirty-nine.

At Olney, he collaborated with poet William Cowper on a collection they wrote and published as *Olney Hymns*. Besides "Amazing Grace," Newton wrote "Safely Through Another Week," the premier English hymn in honor of the Sabbath. He also wrote "How Sweet the Name of Jesus Sounds in a Believer's Ear" and "Glorious Things of Thee Are Spoken, Zion, City of Our God."

John Newton encouraged William Wilberforce in his fight against the slave trade. He introduced Wilberforce to Henry Thorton, who joined the prolonged, but successful, campaign in Parliament to outlaw the slave trade.

He became a highly influential member of that group of clergy within the Anglican communion known as evangelicals and was one of the founders of the Church Missionary Society, which sent out hundreds of evangelical missionaries throughout the next century.

In the beginning, large crowds came to hear Newton preach, but when the American Revolution occurred, he angered people by his pro-American sentiments and became unpopular. He was then offered a parish in London, where he lived until his death at the age of eighty-two.

Sixteen years after the American Declaration of Independence, Princeton University conferred honorary degrees on statesmen Alexander Hamilton and Thomas Jefferson. The same day, it awarded the Doctor of Divinity degree to John Newton, the pastor of a small-town church in rural England.

He arose, and came to his father.
But when he was yet a great way off,
his father saw him, and had compassion, and ran,
and fell on his neck, and kissed him.

Luke 15:20

A Voice in the Slums

Catherine hurried through the dirty streets of London's East End on her way to Gateshead Methodist Chapel to hear her husband preach. Ragged children played in the alleyways, while mangy dogs pawed through garbage. Just ahead of her, a shabbily clad woman sat on the steps of a ramshackle tenement house, a jug in her hand.

Poor, poor woman, Catherine thought. *If only she'd go over to the chapel to hear my husband speak, I'm sure her life would be changed by the power of God.*

"Speak to that woman," a voice said.

Startled, Catherine looked around to see who might have spoken. There was no one except the children and dogs going about their play. Was it her imagination? Or had the Lord spoken? The thought sent chills down her spine.

"No, Lord, I'm afraid," Catherine reasoned. "Besides, she wouldn't listen. She's probably drunk."

"Speak to the woman."

"But, Lord, I'll be late for the meeting," Catherine argued.

"Wouldn't you be doing God more service by inviting her to the chapel than going there yourself?" God seemed to say to her.

Catherine took a deep breath. "All right, Lord, If You say so, I'll try."

Smiling at the woman, Catherine shyly asked, "Would you like to come to the chapel with me?"

The woman sighed and shook her head. "Can't. Got to stay home with my husband. He's drunk." She nodded her head toward the door.

"May I talk to him?" Catherine surprised herself with this question. "Maybe I can help him."

"No use," the woman mumbled. "He's so drunk he'd never hear a word you'd say."

"Please," Catherine persisted. "Let me try. I don't mind that he's drunk and I'm not afraid."

The woman got up then and led her into the small, dark flat to where her husband slumped in a chair, a jug on the floor beside him. He didn't seem to notice their presence.

"Lord, what shall I say?" Catherine sent a quick prayer to God for guidance.

"God loves you!" Catherine spoke with authority. "Listen to me! He loves you so much that He sent Jesus to die on the cross for your sins! He cares about you."

The man turned his eyes toward her and listened intently, as though trying to grasp the truth that God really loved him. Encouraged, Catherine took out her Bible and opened it to Luke 15. Beginning at verse 11, she read the story of the prodigal son.

As she read about the father running to meet his son, tears welled up in the man's bloodshot eyes and trickled down his dirty cheeks.

"God loves you like that father loved his son," Catherine spoke gently. "Now, I want to pray for you."

After the prayer, Catherine promised to come back for a visit to share more of God's love. The man nodded, wiping the tears from his eyes.

Catherine did return, and before long, this man, along with ten other alcoholics, began studying the Bible with her. All ten quit drinking and found a new life in Christ Jesus.

That brief encounter with God's Word was the turning point not only in the drunkard's life, but in Catherine's as well. Awakened to the power of personal contact, she pledged herself to spend two evenings every week visiting systematically from house to house, sharing God's message of love. It strengthened her belief that God can use women as well as men to do His work. It impressed upon her the power of God to change the worst sinners.

Epilogue

After that encounter in London's East End in 1860, Catherine Mumford Booth threw all of her energies into working with her husband, William Booth, for the afflicted, the forgotten, and the downtrodden of society. Together, they founded The Salvation Army. She is known as the "mother of the Salvation Army."

From her first public testimony in 1860 until her death in 1891, she was known as a dynamic, fervent, and forceful speaker. Catherine once said that she felt more at home on the platform than she did in the kitchen. She was a sought-after temperance lecturer, and large crowds turned out to hear her speak at open-air meetings as well as in churches and public halls. On the twenty-fifth anniversary of the Salvation Army, fifty thousand gathered to hear her speak.

Catherine worked not only for alcoholics, but for prostitutes also, establishing London's first Rescue Home for young girls caught in prostitution. She lobbied with government leaders and helped secure the passing of the Criminal Law Amendment Act that was designed to protect teenage girls from prostitution.

According to Norman Murdock, "No man of her era exceeded her in popularity or spiritual results, including her husband."

In her book, *Great Women of the Christian Faith*, Edith Deen commented, "She is remembered for her work in defining the position of women in the Salvation Army and for using their neglected talents. She had extraordinary ability to transform vague religious beliefs into living reality. She stands out as one of the most vital and courageous Christian workers of all time."

When Catherine Booth died, fifty thousand people filed past her casket as she lay in state for five days in London's Congress Hall. Five thousand women officers of the Army were among them, women she had inspired and trained for service. Her eight children all held positions of trust in the organization she helped found.

God be merciful to me a sinner.

Luke 18:13

The Hunchback of Westminster Abbey

The hand that unshackled the African slaves of the British Empire was the hand of a hunchback. Misshapen from birth and stunted in growth, William Wilberforce became one of the most popular political leaders in the British Empire. When his funeral cortege wound its way through crowded streets to Westminster Abbey in 1833, all London seemed to be in mourning.

His statue in the Abbey is an artist's triumph. The seated figure reveals the noble face and fine features of Wilberforce but conceals his frightful physical deformities.

A few days before his death, the bill to abolish slavery in the British colonies passed its final reading in the House of Commons. Wilberforce first lifted his voice against the horrors of African slavery in Parliament forty-four years before. For years he annually introduced a bill in parliament for abolition. It was defeated year after year by the powerful business interests made wealthy by the despicable trade in human flesh.

What mysterious forces within his mind and heart enabled him to endure defeat until victory was finally won and the slave trade was ended and the slaves set free?

When William was only nine, his father, a prosperous merchant, died. His mother sent him to live with his childless aunt and uncle, Hannah and William Wilberforce in Wimbledon. They were friends of the silver-tongued evangelist George Whitefield. William's aunt took him often to hear the evangelical sermons then being preached in the local parish church.

When William wrote his mother about this, she became alarmed that her son might become a Methodist. She hurried by coach to London to save him from such "poison."

Returning to Hull, she made sure he attended the theater, dances, card parties, and fashionable suppers. She sought to give him a taste of the world and its diversions so that his early religious impressions would be stifled. She succeeded! He was captured by the social whirl.

At twenty-one, Wilberforce was elected to Parliament and became a close friend and advisor of the future prime minister, William Pitt. He became noted for his entertaining sense of humor and eloquent oratory.

The biographical writer, James Boswell, described him at a large campaign rally in a cold rain. He watched Wilberforce, barely five feet tall, capture the interest of the bored crowd. He said, "I saw him as a shrimp mount the table, but as I listened the shrimp grew until it became a whale."

When William was 25 years old and had already gained a reputation for his wild parties and popularity in Parliament, he took a vacation trip to France. He invited his former school master Isaac Milner to join him.

On the way, William mocked at the religious enthusiasm of the Methodists. Milner challenged him to read the Scriptures for himself. He agreed and began to read them daily. A subtle change came into his tastes and manners. He no longer enjoyed the party scene. His frivolity disappeared.

A few months later, on another trip, he and Milner read through the Greek New Testament together. A conflict raged inside William. As he drank, danced, and dined at the parties of his friends, William began to feel he was not a real Christian.

His spiritual anguish continued for several months. He felt condemned for having wasted his time and his talents. Finally, under a great sense of despair, William recalled the parable of the Pharisee and the publican.

The words of Luke 18:13 came forcibly to his mind. He made his decision to pray the sinner's prayer, "God be merciful to me a sinner."

Instantly, William's heart was filled with peace. A new joy and sense of purpose entered his life. William Wilberforce was born again!

He never forgot that powerful passage. Almost half a

century later, Joseph Gurney, a Quaker friend, visited him during his final illness. Wilberforce told his friend he had nothing to urge for himself but the poor publican's plea, "God be merciful to me a sinner."

Epilogue

At the time of his conversion, Wilberforce sought the advice of John Newton, the former slave ship captain, then an evangelical minister. Newton counseled him that he should remain in public life and place his political influence at the service of his Saviour.

Wilberforce became spokesman and leader for a group of evangelical Christians who lived at Clapham, near London, several of whom served in public life. They dedicated their energies to numerous reform causes, among them the plight of the poor, the prisoners, and the slaves.

In 1789, Wilberforce first proposed a motion in Parliament for the abolition of the African slave trade. He continued to champion the cause for eighteen years, with the encouragement of his Clapham friends. Finally, in 1807, legislation was passed forbidding British vessels to engage in the trade.

Later, in 1833, legislation was enacted freeing all slaves in the British dominions.

Wilberforce participated in the formation of the British and Foreign Bible Society and the Church Missionary Society. In 1813, he got legislation through Parliament forcing the East India Company to open India to Christian missionaries.

*T*hen said Jesus, "Father, forgive them; for they know not what they do."
Luke 23:34

A Gentleman in Prison

On April 29, 1915, Tokichi Ishii murdered the geisha girl who attended him in a teahouse in Tokyo. So cleverly did he cover his crime that no one suspected him. Later, while in prison on another charge, Tokichi overheard fellow prisoners discussing the teahouse murder. The girl's boyfriend, Komori, had been arrested.

Congratulations! Tokichi told himself. *It doesn't matter that he's innocent. What matters is that you didn't get caught!*

Later, Tokichi began to feel sympathy for Komori and his family. *That's not fair*, he thought. *Why should they suffer for what I did? I will confess my guilt and save the innocent man.*

Following his confession, Tokichi worked tirelessly

to establish Komori's innocence and his own guilt. The trial dragged on for months. It became a great media event in Japan, with multitudes following the reports in the press. Gamblers placed bets on the outcome. Finally, the court issued it's verdict—not guilty.

Tokichi became so agitated over his acquittal that he couldn't sleep. The case was appealed to a higher court. Ishii was sentenced to death. He was delighted! Justice had triumphed!

Miss Caroline MacDonald, a Scottish missionary in Tokyo, determined to share the gospel with Tokichi. On the next New Year's Day, she sent him a special meal, followed with special meals on the second and third days of the New Year. Then she sent him a copy of the New Testament.

Tokichi casually turned the pages without much interest. Then he noticed a passage where Jesus set his face to go to Jerusalem, though death awaited him. He appreciated the Man's courage. When he read how Jesus was declared innocent by Pilate but was executed, Tokichi's sense of justice was aroused. It wasn't right to treat an innocent man this way!

Reading further, Tokichi came to the words of Jesus from the cross, "Father, forgive them." About the impact of that text, he wrote, "I was stabbed to the heart as if pierced by a five-inch nail . . . The last words that a man utters come from the depths of his soul; he does not die with a lie upon his lips . . . So I cannot but believe that (these final words of Jesus) reveal His true heart."

Tokichi felt those words were for him. There in the prison cell, he accepted Jesus and received His forgiveness.

In his own words, "My unspeakably hardened heart was changed, and I repented of all my crimes. Such power is not in man."

Epilogue

In the time between his conversion and his execution, Tokishi Ishii kept a diary. One day he wrote, "In this narrow cell, nine feet by six, I am happier than if I were living in the largest house I ever saw. The joy of each day is very great. These things are all due to the grace and favor of Jesus." His last words were a poem of faith in life beyond the grave. Miss MacDonald received his books and manuscripts and published his story.

In the beginning was the Word,
and the Word was with God,
and the Word was God.
John 1:1

Discovery in a Barn

It was a hot, humid day in August. University student Boris Dotsenko was visiting his grandfather's farm in the Ukraine to recover from a recent bout of pneumonia. Boris wandered into an old barn to get out of the sun and fell asleep on a pile of hay.

While he slept, he rolled down between the hay and the rough wooden back wall of the barn. Awaking, he struggled to right himself, but only slid farther down the pile of hay ending up on the floor. Coughing and sputtering from the dust he'd stirred up, Boris looked around for a way out.

At his feet, Boris noticed a pile of old papers. There were some copies of an old magazine which he cast aside. Under them was an old book without a cover.

Boris picked it up and leafed through its yellowed pages.

On the left was something written in a language Boris couldn't understand, but he recognized it as Old Slavonic script. *Interesting!* Boris thought. *I wonder what it says?*

Glancing to the right, he saw that it was a Russian translation. He read, "The gospel of Our Lord Jesus Christ . . ."

His heart beat rapidly as he held what he knew was a forbidden book, the Christian Bible. At that time, shortly after World War II, Christianity was frowned upon in his country. Churches were closed; many of them had been burned. Thousands of Christians had been sent to Siberia for their faith. Although he knew that what he was doing was a crime, Boris hid the Bible in his shirt and sneaked it into his room.

Closing the door, he pulled the Bible out of his shirt and began to read, "In the beginning was the Word, and the Word was with God, and the Word was God."

This is the exact opposite of everything I've been taught, Boris told himself as he continued to read. *I'm an atheist. I should report this find to the authorities.*

However, his curiosity got the better of him. He read it again, shocked by its words and frightened at the way they made him feel. *I must read more!* Boris promised himself and hid the book under his mattress.

For two weeks, Boris spent a lot of time in his room, reading that old Bible. He discovered several sayings there, words of Jesus, that he had been taught were the words of Stalin. Then one day when he reached for the book, it was gone.

"To this day I know neither how nor why it happened," Boris writes, "but what I read had left its mark on me."

Boris couldn't forget the words he had read. They followed him when he returned to the University in Kiev and later to the University of Leningrad where he studied for his master's degree in physics and mathematics.

While in Leningrad, he discovered another Bible in an unexpected place—in the study of one of his professors, Dr. Jakov Frenkel. With the realization that there were scientists who were unafraid to have faith in the Bible, Boris began praying for God to guide him to truth.

After receiving his Ph.D. from Moscow State University, Boris returned to Kiev where he worked as a nuclear physicist. After becoming the head of his laboratory, he was sent to the University of Alberta, Canada, on a fact-finding mission. Following that, he was to go to Vienna where he would be a member of the International Atomic Energy Agency. A brilliant future lay ahead of him. There was talk by his colleagues that he might be nominated for the Nobel Prize in Physics.

Boris was put up at a motel in Edmonton. While unpacking, he noticed a Bible on the bedside stand, placed there by the Gideons. With trembling hands, he lifted the precious book and leafed through it's crisp white pages. It fell open to John 1:1. Once again Boris read, "In the beginning was the Word, and the Word was God."

Into his mind flashed the memory of sitting in the

hay in his grandfather's barn many years before reading those same words from yellowed pages in Russian.

By now, Boris was ready to accept its words as truth.
He had been doing a lot of thinking about one of the
fundamental laws of nature, the Law of Entropy. Simply stated, this law says that if left to itself, any physical
system will decay with time. *According to that law,
our planet should have turned into dust long, long ago!*
Boris reasoned. *There must be something very powerful that is keeping that from happening. This must be
God. Yes, there has to be a God in heaven holding everything together!*

Every spare moment Boris spent in his motel room
in Edmonton reading the Gideon Bible. The words of
Scripture burned their way into his heart. Boris became
a Christian and was baptized.

Epilogue

Dr. Boris P. Dotsenko asked for political asylum in
Canada in 1966. Since then, he has taught physics at
Waterloo Lutheran University in Waterloo, Ontario, and
the University of Toronto.

About his journey from atheism to Christianity, Boris
comments, "I thank Him for bringing to my attention
three times, in different places and over many years,
His book for the world, the Bible. And I thank Him too
for granting me the faith to know him personally and to
experience His love."

*There cometh a woman of Samaria
to draw water:
Jesus saith unto her,
Give me to drink.*

John 4:7

Hindu Woman at the Well

Pandita Ramabai, a Hindu Brahmin, walked thousands of miles on pilgrimages in India and traveled halfway around the world before she found Christ through a powerful encounter with God's Word.

Ramabai's father was a Chitpawan Brahmin, the highest caste in southern India. He was a teacher of Sanskrit and the Hindu scriptures. He also taught these to Ramabai, the study of which was forbidden to all women. For this, his family was ostracized and reduced to poverty. By the time she was twelve, Ramabai could recite 18,000 verses from the Hindu scriptures. She understood Sanskrit and was fluent in Marathi, Kannada, Hindi, and Bengali.

Ramabai traveled with her father, mother, older sister, and brother thousands of miles, criss-crossing India to visit temples and holy shrines seeking merit. During the Madras famine of 1876-77, both parents and her older sister died. Before he died, her father admonished Ramabai, "Remember to seek the way of righteousness. I have given you into the hand of our God; you are His, and to Him alone you must belong and serve Him all your life."

After the death of her parents, Ramabai continued wandering India with her brother seeking spiritual peace. By the time they reached Calcutta, faith in their father's idols was shaken, and they were seeking a new path. About this time, they were invited by a converted Brahmin to attend a Christian youth gathering.

Ramabai found the Christian service meaningless. She was puzzled to see them kneeling, talking to their chairs. *What strange people Christians are*, she thought. *They have no gods, but pray to their chairs.*

After the death of her brother, she married a close friend of his, a lawyer. He died of cholera after nine months. She wrote, "This great grief drew me nearer to God. I felt He was teaching me, and that if I was to come to Him, He must Himself draw me."

In her husband's library, she discovered Luke's gospel and began to read it. A missionary visited her often and explained the teachings of Christianity. She felt especially drawn to its teaching that all people, regardless of caste or gender, are equal. About this time, she became greatly concerned for the thousands of child widows who were treated as slaves or driven to prostitution. She left for England to seek a solution.

In England, Ramabai enrolled in Cheltenham Ladies' College. While studying there, she visited a home for fallen women run by Christian women. "What makes you care for these girls with such tenderness?" Ramabai wanted to know.

Her guide opened the Bible to John 4 and read her the story of Christ's encounter with the Samaritan woman. "Christ's love for sinners is infinite," the woman explained. "He is the divine Saviour of the world, of all people, no matter how far they have fallen."

There in the Bible, in the story of Jesus and the woman at the well, Pandita Ramabai realized she had come face to face with the God she had been seeking. She saw herself and all the women of India in that woman at the well. Here was the truth she had been longing to find.

About this encounter with Christ, she wrote, "I realized, after reading the 4th Chapter of St. John's gospel, that Christ was truly the Divine Saviour He claimed to be, and no one but He could transform and uplift the downtrodden womanhood of India and of every land."

Ramabai returned to India a baptized, committed Christian. Today, she is known as the founder of Mukti Mission at Kedgaon, Poona District, India, a center of hope for women. By many she is considered to be India's greatest woman of the past century.

POWERFUL PASSAGES

Epilogue

In 1889, upon her return to India after travels in England and the United States seeking supporters, she opened a school for women, with one child-widow as her first student. Eleven years later, she was caring for 1,900 girls and women that she had gathered from all over India, 650 of them under the age of fourteen, orphans and child-widows.

After reading the faith methods of George Mueller and Hudson Taylor, she adopted their policy of asking God to supply all their needs. She once wrote, "I am literally penniless with no means of any kind. I own nothing on earth but a few clothes and my Bible. . . . I am poor and needy, yet the Lord thinketh upon me. His resources are limitless, and He has promised to supply all my needs."

Another time she wrote, "I feel very happy since the Lord called me to step out in faith, and I obeyed. . . . We are not rich, nor great, but we are happy, getting our daily bread directly from the loving hands of our Heavenly Father, having not a pice (smallest Indian coin) over and above our daily necessities, having no banking account anywhere, no endowment or income from any earthly source, but depending altogether on our father God. . . . The Lord is our Inexhaustible Treasure."

Ramabai spent the last fifteen years of her life translating the Bible from the Greek and Hebrew into Marathi. The type was set and Bibles printed by the women of Mukti Mission. This is the only Bible in the history of the church that is entirely the work of women, the only one translated completely by a woman. She was very ill during the final proofreading of this Bible in 1922. She knew her end was near, but she prayed, "Lord keep me going long enough to finish the proofreading." Ten days later, the completed manuscript was ready to print. She died the same day—April 5, 1922.

*He that heareth my word,
and believeth on him that sent me,
hath everlasting life.*

John 5:24

Born Walking

It was Friday night. Twenty-year-old Dawson Trotman sat in a police cruiser on the way to jail. Moments before, he'd been arrested while staggering down a street looking for his car. *This will kill Mom when she hears about it*, he thought. *I know she's at home praying for me.*

The policeman broke into his thoughts, "Do you like this kind of life?"

"No way!" Dawson shook his head. "I hate it." And in that moment, he hated everything about his life: his lying, gambling, stealing, smoking, drinking, and dancing. The glamor was gone. He longed for something better.

The policeman took him to a park to allow him to

sober up in the fresh air. After three hours, the police-man asked, "If I let you go now, do you think you can straighten out your life."

"I'll try," Dawson promised. "I'll try real hard."

On Sunday, Dawson showed up at the youth meeting in his church. There was quite a bit of excitement about a scripture memorizing contest. *I can win that!* Dawson told himself, and he did. He was the only one to learn all ten texts the leader assigned. The next week he learned another ten.

By the third week, he'd forgotten his promise to the policeman and had returned to his old way of life, drink-ing every night in the tavern.

One morning as he walked to work, one of the twenty verses he had learned came to mind with sudden force, "He that heareth my word, and believeth on him that sent me, hath everlasting life."*Wow!* Dawson thought. *Imagine that! Everlasting life! That's wonderful! Lord, I'd sure like to have it! How do I get it?*

As though it were God answering his question, the words of another memory verse flashed into his mind, "But as many as received him, to them gave he power to become the sons of God."

"OK, God," Dawson responded. "I'm not sure what it means to receive Jesus, but I'll do that right now!" He walked the rest of the way to work with a song in his heart, sensing that his old life was now gone forever. Dawson was born again on the way to work.

Epilogue

Immediately, Dawson began memorizing one new Bible verse every day. Within three years, he had more than a thousand texts memorized. Seven years later, in 1933, Dawson founded The Navigators, a parachurch organization that witnessed, at first, to sailors. It later became a worldwide organization, teaching the basic principles of Christian growth: Bible study, prayer, witnessing, and fellowship.

*S*earch the scriptures;
for in them ye think ye have eternal life:
and they are they which testify of me.
John 5:39

The Barefoot Seeker

Bibles were scarce in Wales in 1794. The available few were so expensive that only the wealthy could afford one. The Jones family was poor, but that did not stop Mary from reading the Bible.

One day, Mary walked two miles to a neighbor's home and timidly asked, "Please, may I read your Bible for just a little while? I promise to be very careful with it."

"Of course, my child," the farmer's wife replied. "Come in." She led Mary into the best room of the house where the Bible sat in a place of honor on a polished table. A crisp white cloth covered the precious book. "Take as long as you like," the woman said. Slipping quietly out, she left Mary alone with a Bible for the first time in her life.

Breathless with excitement, Mary lifted the cloth and

placed it on the table beside her. With trembling hands, she opened the large book. By chance it fell open to John 5. There she read the words of Jesus, "Search the scriptures."

"Yes, Lord, I will! I will!" Mary cried. "Oh, if only I had a Bible of my own!"

On her walk home that day, Mary planned how she could earn money enough for a Bible of her own. She would clean houses, cook, wash, sew, or do chores—anything to earn money for the Word.

Six years later, Mary had enough money. She walked barefoot twenty-eight miles to the town of Bala, where she had heard there were Welsh Bibles for sale. She went straight to the home of Pastor Thomas Charles, who had the only copies then available.

"I've come to buy a Bible," Mary said simply.

"I am so sorry," Pastor Charles said. "All of the Bibles I have are already reserved. I have no idea when we will have more."

Tears spilled down Mary's cheeks. "Do you mean I have worked and saved for six years for nothing?" she sobbed. Covering her face with her hands, Mary cried as though her heart would break. As Pastor Charles watched her, tears filled his eyes too.

"You shall have a Bible," he said, handing her one of the reserved copies. "Someone else will have to wait."

Epilogue

Two years later, Pastor Charles told Mary Jones's story

in London and pleaded for a society to be formed to print and circulate Welsh Bibles. "Why not for the whole world?" someone else suggested. So it was that the British and Foreign Bible Society was formed on March 7, 1804.

im that cometh to me
I will in no wise cast out.
John 6:37

A Musty Old Book

"Yes, Lord, I will go," he said, but he never went. The man who had the greatest impact on the involvement of American and Canadian evangelical churches in foreign missions in the early part of the twentieth century never was a foreign missionary himself!

Albert Simpson was born of Scottish stock in Prince Edward Island, Canada. He lived in a committed Christian home, but he had no personal hope in Christ. His father was a disciplined church presbyter, but Albert's strict religious training failed to give him an understanding of the simple gospel of Jesus.

One day in the library of an elderly minister and teacher, Albert happened upon a musty old book. Turning the pages, he read a sentence that opened the gates of eternal life to him. It quoted John 6:37, "Him that cometh to me I will in no wise cast out." The book declared that the moment you come to Jesus in simple faith, you pass from death to life and receive forgiveness for all your sins.

Immediately, Albert fell to his knees and prayed, "Lord Jesus, Thou hast said, 'Him that cometh to me I will in no wise cast out.' Thou knowest how long and earnestly I have tried to come, but I did not know how. Now I come the best I can, and I dare to believe that Thou dost receive me and save me, and that I am now Thy child, forgiven and saved simply because I have taken Thee at Thy word."

Epilogue

Albert studied for the ministry in Knox College, Toronto. Later, while pastoring a large church in Louisville, Kentucky, he had a deeper spiritual experience. At that time, he felt God was calling him to go to China as a missionary.

Albert promised to go, but his wife, the mother of his six children, refused! As time passed, he became convinced that he could labor for the world and those perishing out of Christ just the same as if he were permitted to go among them.

Albert moved to New York and in 1887 organized the Christian and Missionary Alliance. He launched the first illustrated missions journal and conducted interdenominational mission rallies throughout North America. By

1902, his organization had 150 missionaries working in fifteen foreign fields.

He is reported to have opened over four hundred stations in sixteen different countries. Several faith mission organizations, such as the Sudan Interior Mission and the Africa Inland Mission were begun by graduates of his school.

Simpson opened a missionary training school at Nyack, New York, which inspired the Bible Institute movement, a major source of recruits for independent faith mission societies.

Through A. B. Simpson's influence, many North American evangelical churches made foreign missions a top priority. He wrote seventy books and over three hundred hymns.

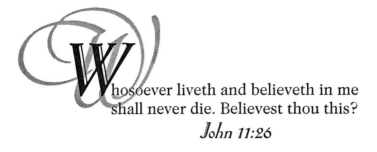 hosoever liveth and believeth in me
shall never die. Believest thou this?

John 11:26

An Agnostic
Finds Christ

Audrey was confused. She no longer believed the Christian faith, but neither could she accept atheism. While studying secular philosophy in France, she had given up her belief in the Bible but she had nothing to fill the vacuum that remained.

I guess I'm an agnostic, Audrey reasoned. *I'm not sure there is a God, but then again, I'm not sure there isn't.*

Life held no meaning. *If it is true that there is no life beyond this one on earth, then what does it matter how I live now? If this is all there is to life, then why work so hard to make a better world?* Such thoughts troubled Audrey for months.

One night, Audrey locked herself in her bedroom, determined to discover what she believed. Not bothering to turn on a light, she went to the window and threw it open. Looking up at the heavens she cried out, "God, if there be a God, if You will give me some philosophy that makes reasonable sense to me, I will commit myself to follow it."

She paced the bedroom floor mulling over the philosophies she had studied in college. Then the words of Jesus came clearly to her mind, "Whosoever liveth and believeth in me shall never die. Believest thou this?"

Of course not! Audrey thought. *I've already settled that question. Bible stories don't make sense. I can't believe those miracle stories—the virgin birth, Jonah and the whale, and Noah and the Flood. The Bible is not reasonable.*

"Whosoever liveth and believeth in me shall never die. Believest thou this?" She could not get those words out of her mind. *Could it really be true that Jesus Christ lived and died that we might have eternal life? I sure wish this were true, that this world isn't the end, that there is something beyond,* Audrey thought wistfully.

Then in her words, "Suddenly God's mysterious revelation was given to me. I could not reason out the mystery of the incarnation, but God caused me to know that this was a fact. I knelt in tears of joy and worshipped him as Saviour and Lord."

Epilogue
Audrey Wetherell Johnson served with the China Inland Mission as a teacher for fourteen years until forced

to leave China in 1950 due to the political situation. In 1958, she founded Bible Study Fellowship, now located in San Antonio, Texas, an international organization that promotes disciplined and personal Bible study. In her life, she inspired thousands to accept the authority of God's Word for their lives.

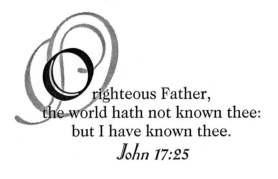

O righteous Father,
the world hath not known thee:
but I have known thee.
John 17:25

Night of Fire

When holidays approach, most of us turn to media weather forecasts so we can best plan our leisure activity. When we do, we are indebted to a child prodigy of seventeenth-century France named Blaise Pascal. In 1648, Pascal directed experiments with a mercury tube on a mountainside five thousand feet above the town of Clermont-Ferrand that established the principle of the barometer.

When we travel by air, we are indebted to him. Those same experiments provided the basis for the altimeter that measures the distance airplanes fly above the airport.

When we use the hydraulic braking systems in our cars, we are indebted to Pascal for his discovery of

"Pascal's Law of Hydrostatics." His law stated the principle that makes all modern hydraulic operations possible.

Pascal invented the first workable calculating machine to help his father do his daily reports as a tax collector. His ideas form the basis of our modern calculators, odometers, speedometers, fare registers, and even computers.

His father, a scientist and committed Christian, taught his son that faith in God was his most valuable possession. From the time Pascal was eighteen, he suffered from a nervous disease that daily gave him great pain.

When he was twenty-eight, Pascal's father died, and he found himself rich and on his own. He took an expensive home, staffed it with many servants, and drove about Paris with his own coach behind four or six horses. Turning from piety to pleasure, he enjoyed the company of witty men and pretty women in games and diversions. Some of their discussions led him to religious doubt.

But his younger sister, whom he deeply loved, rebuked Pascal for his frivolity and prayed for his reform.

Then one day as he drove across the Neuilly bridge in Paris, his four horses became frightened and plunged off the parapet into the Seine River. Fortunately, the harness broke, or Pascal would have plunged to his death in the river. The carriage was left hanging over the edge.

This frightening experience caused Pascal to reexamine his life's priorities. On the evening of November

23, 1654, he was reading from John 17. God spoke powerfully to him that night through verse 25, "O righteous Father, the world hath not known thee: but I have known thee."

Between 6:30 p.m. and 12:30 a.m., Pascal experienced a vivid personal encounter with God that was very real and meaningful. He felt God speaking personally to his heart and made a full surrender of himself to the Lord. This was his "night of fire."

He wrote out this conversion experience on a piece of parchment which he sewed into the lining of his coat. From that night on, he kept it always on his person. His servant discovered it ten years after his death.

He titled his prayer, "Fire." He used the word "fire" as a symbol for the presence of God, such as in Moses and the burning bush, Isaiah and the coals of fire, and the tongues of fire at Pentecost. Here in part is his prayer written the night the fire of God's presence filled his soul:

"Righteous Father the world hath not known Thee; but I have known Thee.
Joy, joy, joy, tears of joy . . .
I have separated myself from Him
Let me not be separated from Him eternally.
Jesus Christ.
Jesus Christ.
I have separated myself from Him. I have fled from Him,

denied Him, crucified Him.

Let me never be separated from Him.

Total submission to Jesus Christ and to my director.

Eternally in joy for a day's training on earth."

Epilogue

After his conversion, Pascal turned his talents to the defense of the Christian faith. In 1658, he began an *Apology for the Christian Religion,* a brilliant work which was interrupted by his death from cancer at thirty-nine. It argues powerfully for vital Christianity as opposed to skepticism and rationalism.

He lists prophecies, miracles, and history as evidences for the Christian faith. He also believed that the way the Bible proves itself true in the life of the believer is an overwhelming evidence of the validity of Scripture. He believed that God is best known in the believer's heart. He wrote, "The heart has its reasons which reason does not know."

Further scientific inventions of Pascal's included the omnibus in 1662, a horse-drawn wagon that gave Paris the first public system of mass transportation. He is also credited with inventing the first wristwatch.

Modern life insurance tables are based upon Pascal's calculus of probabilities, which he developed when a gambler challenged him to formulate the mathematics of chance.

His law of hydrostatics assisted in the development

of dynamos, turbines, hydraulic pumps, hydraulic jacks, vacuum pumps, air compressors, hydraulic elevators, home-heating systems, air conditioners, and boilers.

One biographer wrote about Pascal, "Pascal belongs to that rare circle of creative souls who cram several lifetimes into a few fleeting years. Mathematician, physicist, philosopher, theologian, and litterateur, he achieved fame in all these areas within a period of about twenty years."

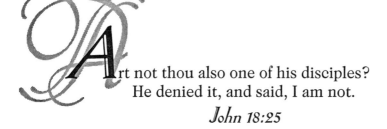

rt not thou also one of his disciples?
He denied it, and said, I am not.

John 18:25

The Scottish
Sword-bearer

John Knox studied in the university at Saint Andrews, Scotland, and was ordained a priest in 1536. While tutoring the sons of Scottish landowners, Knox heard ideas about the need for reformation in the church.

Cardinal David Beaton, newly come from France, was tightening up the discipline of the church in Scotland. In 1544, he had five people executed for such crimes as dishonoring the virgin and eating a goose on a fast day. It was not difficult for the Scots to gain the young tutor's sympathies against such horrors.

Then the plague visited Dundee. People died like flies. A charismatic Protestant preacher named George Wishart prayed for the city and preached Christ to the dying.

When Wishart arrived at Leith near Edinburg, John

Knox was in the crowd that welcomed him. When Wishart stepped ashore, he gave his heavy two-handed sword to John Knox to carry.

For several weeks, Knox carried that sword and served as Wishart's bodyguard. Then sensing that his end was near, Wishart sent Knox back to his pupils with the word, "One is sufficient for a sacrifice." At midnight, Wishart was captured and turned over to Cardinal Beaton. He was tied to a stake, strangled, and burned.

Wishart's death was a great shock to Knox. He felt very guilty for not staying to protect him. At that very time, he was studying the passage in John 18:25 relating Jesus' arrest in Gethsemane. Peter drew a sword to protect Him, but Jesus ordered him to put it away and allowed Himself to be arrested. Later that night, Peter denied Jesus three times.

As Knox studied this passage, he was struck by the close parallel to his experience. Troubled by Peter's denial of Jesus to save himself, he determined not to do a repeat of Peter's mistake. As he studied this powerful passage, John Knox made a fundamental commitment of his life to Jesus Christ. It was there that the future leader of the reformation in Scotland was born again. Years later on his deathbed in 1581, Knox asked his wife, "Go read again where I cast my first anchor!" She read to him John 18:25-27.

Epilogue
Shortly after his conversion, John Knox joined the Protestants who were occupying the castle, in Saint

Andrews and became their spokesman. The French captured the castle and Knox, with others, became a galley slave for two years. Freed by the intervention of England, he preached there for two years, gaining a reputation as a radical Protestant.

At the accession of Queen Elizabeth to the throne of England, Knox returned to Scotland. He led the rebellion against Mary, Queen of Scots, and under his leadership the Scottish Parliament made Presbyterianism the state religion in 1560. From then until his death in 1572, he was considered Scotland's most powerful political and religious leader.

After this, Jesus knowing that all things
were now accomplished,
that the scripture might be fulfilled,
saith, I thirst.

John 19:28

Thirsty No More

A strange new thing happened near Bristol, England, on Saturday, February 17, 1739. George Whitefield, barred by prejudice from preaching in the churches, decided to preach in the out-of-doors!

As the coal miners returned from their pits, Whitefield lifted his voice and shouted, "Blessed are the poor in spirit." As a crowd of 200 gathered, he told a story that made them laugh. Then, holding their attention, he spoke of the cross and the love of God, brushing tears from his own eyes. Soon he noticed the white "gutters" formed by the tears running down the miners' blackened cheeks as he spoke of Jesus, the Friend of sinners.

From then on, open-fields' preaching became a prominent feature of the revival that swept England and

America in the eighteenth century, led by the Wesleys and George Whitefield.

As a traveling preacher, Whitefield spoke more than 15,000 times to literally millions of people on both sides of the Atlantic.

Benjamin Franklin, who had listened to him at an outdoor meeting in Philadelphia, calculated that Whitefield could be heard clearly by up to 30,000 people at one time without any amplification of his voice. He often preached to 20,000 at once.

The great actor, David Garrick, went to hear the same sermon by Whitefield forty times! He said that Whitefield could sway an audience just in the way he said "Mesopotamia." Garrick said he would give 100 guineas to be able to say "Oh" the way that preacher did!

Revivals broke out wherever Whitefield preached, and tens of thousands were converted through his ministry. Whitefield preached hundreds of times on the new birth; it was his favorite topic. He said he knew the time and the place where he experienced that gift from God and urged all to accept it.

It was at Oxford University that Whitefield experienced the power of the new birth after painfully seeking it for months. Afterward, he could hardly speak of anything else; so great was his joy!

When Whitefield was twenty-one years old, Charles Wesley, the hymn writer, loaned him a copy of *The Life of God in the Soul of Man* by Henry Scougal. Reading that work, Whitefield concluded that "true religion is the union of the soul with God." From that moment, he realized that he must be born again. He started to seek that experience by his own works.

First, he tried to be more humble. He stopped powdering his hair, the grooming custom of his day. When his college gown tore on a nail, he did not have it mended, thinking that would make him more humble. He gave up tasty food, such as fruit. He decided that he must deny himself the pleasure of laughter to be united with Christ! He became sick, lost weight, spent hours in prayer, but received no satisfaction.

The only pleasure Whitefield enjoyed at this time was the fellowship of his religious friends in the "Holy Club" at Oxford. He gave up meeting with them. He looked for other sacrifices he could make that might bring on the experience of a new birth.

Whitefield's family thought him out of his mind. For six months, he continued his painful sacrifices. He denied himself adequate clothing and the warmth of a fire on cold days.

When Lent season came, he fasted more rigorously. He gave himself to reciting prayers and collapsed on his bed unable to get up. A physician drew blood from him. For three weeks, he was unable to get off his bed. He devoted all his strength to prayer and reading the New Testament.

While meditating upon the crucifixion of Christ, he remembered how, on the cross, Jesus became thirsty.

He thought of how the water that he drank left his own mouth dry. That brought to mind Jesus' words on the cross recorded in John 19:28, "I thirst." Suddenly, he realized that when Jesus cried out, "I thirst," His sufferings were nearly over!

Whitefield threw himself on his bed and cried out, "I thirst! I thirst!"

All previous prayer had been a conscious attempt to merit God's favor. This was his first cry of utter helplessness. He had ceased to struggle, he had simply believed. From that moment, he felt that he was born again. For the first time in a year, he was happy—incredibly happy—filled with joy and peace.

In Whitefield's own words, "For some time I could not avoid singing psalms wherever I was; but my joy gradually became more settled, and, blessed be God, has abode and increased in my soul, saving a few casual intermissions, ever since."

Epilogue

George Whitefield became the leading figure in the eighteenth century American revival known as the Great Awakening. He is known as the founder of American Revivalism.

In 1740, Whitefield made a six-week preaching tour of New England. He preached 175 times in forty-five days to tens of thousands of people, setting the colonies ablaze with revival.

He crossed the Atlantic thirteen times, to and from

the American colonies, when the sailing could take as much as three months. He made fourteen visits to Scotland and preached in Wales and Ireland, as well as throughout England.

Whitefield founded an orphanage in Georgia in 1738. He was directly involved in the founding of Princeton University, the University of Pennsylvania, and Dartmouth. George Whitefield died in Newbury Port, Massachusetts, in 1770, in his fifty-sixth year.

When Jesus therefore had received
the vinegar, he said, It is finished:
and he bowed his head, and gave up the ghost.

John 19:30

Forgiveness in a Hayloft

Hudson Taylor was a sickly child, unable to attend school except for a brief time. He received most of his education at home. Family Bible reading with prayer was an important practice in the Taylor home. His father was a pharmacist and Methodist lay preacher.

When he was fifteen, Hudson went to work as a bank clerk in a reputable local firm. An older clerk laughed at what he considered Hudson's outdated spiritual views. A free thinker himself, he tried to convince Hudson to share his skeptical attitude toward the authority of the Bible and his doubts about the Christian faith.

Hudson was attracted to these views and began to harbor doubts himself. Concerned, his parents began to pray for him. After only nine months at the bank, an inflammation in his eyes forced him to resign. He returned home to become an apprentice in his father's drugstore.

In June of 1849, seventeen-year-old Hudson was home alone. His father was working, and his mother was out of town on an extensive visit to a friend about eighty miles distant. He was bored and looked around the house for something to read to pass the time. While looking through his father's library, he discovered some tracts.

Hudson smiled as he chose one of them. *The stories in these tracts are usually interesting*, he thought. *I'll read the stories and skip the spiritual lesson that always comes at the end.* He didn't realize he was about to be hit with the lesson this time right in the middle of the story!

Hudson took the tract out to the barn, climbed up into the hayloft, made himself comfortable, and began to read. The story was of a sick coal man who was in anguish because he thought his sins prevented him from reaching Christ. Some friends visited and encouraged him that Christ had already borne his sins with Him to Calvary.

Suddenly the worried coal man shouted, "Then it's done! My sins are gone!"

Those words hit Taylor with unexpected force. Suddenly, the statement of Jesus on the cross rushed powerfully into his mind, "It is finished."

Light flashed into Hudson's soul as he realized, *Christ's finished work on the cross is for me, Hudson Taylor. There is nothing for me to do to make myself better. I should simply trust the work of Christ on my behalf. My sins are already forgiven. All I need to do is to repent and believe.* Right there and then, Hudson fell to his knees and accepted Jesus as his Saviour.

What he did not know until later was that for the past month his sister had prayed daily for his conversion.

Nor did he know that his mother that very day had gone to her room determined to pray for her son until she had the assurance that he had found Christ. She remained on her knees for several hours, until the Holy Spirit gave her peace in her heart that all was well with Hudson.

When Mrs. Taylor arrived home two weeks later, Hudson met her at the door. "I've some glad news for you, Mother," he said, smiling broadly.

"I know, my boy; I have been rejoicing for a fortnight in the glad tidings you have to tell me," she replied. Then she told him of her all day prayer vigil. She had been on her knees while he read the tract in the hayloft.

Epilogue

Soon after his conversion in the hayloft, Hudson Taylor came under the conviction that God was calling him to China, to the vast inland empire where no missionary had ever gone. At that time, missionaries were allowed only in the five treaty ports but were excluded from the inland provinces.

Interestingly, before Hudson's birth, his father had prayed that if he should be given a son, that he would be called to be a missionary in China!

Taylor studied medicine and the Chinese language and sailed for China in 1853 at the age of twenty-one. He was forced to return home because of poor health. While walking along the beach at Brighton, England, in June of 1865, he prayed for twenty-four missionaries: two for each unentered province in China. Within a year, he had them and returned to China, beginning the China Inland Mission. He taught his missionaries to take local occupations and to rely on no mission board for their financial needs but to rely on God alone through prayer.

Later, Taylor prayed for seventy and then one hundred missionaries. He accepted missionaries from the working classes, not waiting for the educated or for ordained ministers. Many of the recruits were single women that no other missionary organization would accept. Their mission was nondenominational, and volunteers came from several denominations in Britain and North America.

By 1845, the China Inland Mission was the largest single Protestant body in China. During the Boxer Uprising in 1900, ninety-one of his missionaries were brutally murdered in Shansi Province alone. Taylor's health never recovered that tragedy. He died in 1905, leaving 205 stations in China with 849 missionaries and 125,000 Chinese believers.

China watchers in Hong Kong estimate that there were between twenty-five and sixty-six million Christians in China in 1995. Much of the vitality of Christian faith in China today can be traced to the pioneering work of J. Hudson Taylor and the China Inland Mission.

*And they said,
Believe on the Lord Jesus Christ,
and thou shalt be saved, and thy house.*

Acts 16:31

How the Burglar Got Caught!

Valentine Burke was a burglar. By the time he was forty years old, he had spent twenty years behind bars. He was known to the police in St. Louis, Missouri, as one of the worst characters in the city.

When world-famous evangelist Dwight L. Moody came to preach in St. Louis in 1880, Burke the burglar was in jail awaiting trial on a serious charge.

The *Globe-Democrat* newspaper published verbatim reports of Moody's sermons each day. The morning after Moody preached on the apostle Paul's imprisonment at Philippi, the midnight earthquake, and the conversion of the jailer, its headline read: "How the Jailer at Philippi Was Caught!"

The jailer threw a copy of the newspaper into Valentine Burke's cell. That headline caught his eye. "Say . . ." he said half out loud. "Philippi? Hmmm! That's a little town over near Chicago. I know that town. I know that jail. I know that jailer. He's a nasty fellow. I wonder what rap they got him on?"

Burke picked up the paper and began to read. He was interested in the story, until it dawned on him, *This is an old story, not a news story. How disgusting! What's the date on this thing? Well, look at that! It has today's date. Why are they printing such stale news? Something funny's going on here.*

He continued to read until he came to Moody's appeal. Then he threw the paper down in disgust. But the words of Moody's text, "Believe on the Lord Jesus Christ, and thou shalt be saved," stuck in his mind.

Burke could not shake off the conviction that he was a lost man. He realized that he was responsible before God for his evil career. The thought of the jailer at Philippi facing death without God plagued his thoughts all day.

That night, Burke couldn't sleep. At midnight, a church clock struck twelve. He thought of Moody's newspaper message again, half expecting God to send an earthquake to shake his prison cell and bring him to repentance.

A powerful conviction came upon Burke. He knelt down and prayed for the first time in his life. He shed bitter tears as he pleaded with God to forgive the awful record of his life. At that moment, a mysterious, wonderful peace flooded his soul. He picked up the paper and in a sliver of moonlight read again the promise of God. He bowed again in prayer. This time, his tears were tears of joy, for the awful burden of guilt had been removed from him.

When the jailer brought his breakfast, Burke greeted him with a cheerful, "Good morning, sir!"

Surprised at such unexpected courtesy, the jailer asked, "What's gotten into you?"

"I met the Lord Jesus Christ in my cell last night. I'm a new man this morning!"

Hmmph, thought the jailer, *I've seen jailhouse repentance before. We'll see how long this one lasts.*

When Burke's case came to trial, the court did not prosecute with enthusiasm, and he was let off on a legal technicality.

Burke traveled east to New York City and back but was unable to secure a regular job because of his criminal record. He thought it was because of his "ugly face" and prayed that the Lord would make him better-looking.

One day, the sheriff in St. Louis summoned him to the courthouse. Burke worried, *They must be charging me with an old case. Anyway, if I'm guilty, I'll admit it. I've done with lying.*

The sheriff greeted him with a smile. "Where have you been, Burke?"

"In New York."

"What have you been doing there?"

"Trying to find an honest job."

"Have you kept a good grip on your religion?"

"Yes, sheriff, I've had a hard time, but I haven't lost my religion."

"Burke," continued the sheriff, "I've had you shadowed ever since you left jail. I suspected your religion was a fraud. But I am convinced now that you are sincere. You've lived an honest life. I sent for you to offer you a position as my deputy. You can begin at once."

During the next ten years, every deputy was changed except Burke. Finally, they appointed the ex-con as treasurer of the sheriff's office.

Epilogue

Burke, the criminal, had an ugly pock-marked face. Seven years after his conversion, he had a fresh photograph taken. He was so impressed with the contrast between it and the one in the police files that he sent them both to D. L. Moody in Chicago with the comment: "Notice the difference in the enclosed pictures. See what our holy religion can do for the chief of sinners."

Burke inscribed the words of Psalm 113:7, 8 on the back of his rogue's gallery photo: "He raiseth up the poor out of the dust, and lifteth the needy out of the dunghill; that he may set him with princes, even with the princes of his people."

He continued as the treasurer of the sheriff's office until his death in 1895, leading an active, consistent, Christian life.

*For therein is the righteousness of God
revealed from faith to faith:
as it is written, The just shall live by faith.*

Romans 1:17

Voice on the Staircase

"O Lord, save me!" Martin cried out in anguish. "Save me from this storm and I will become a monk!"

The year was 1505. Twenty-two-year-old Martin Luther was walking from his home in Mansfeld, Germany, to the law school in Erfurt when a storm struck.

Lightning flashed, thunder roared, and rain came down in sheets that drove him to seek shelter under the nearest tree. The wind tore at his clothing and broke off tree limbs as he crouched in the darkness. Suddenly, a jagged bolt of lightning jolted the earth nearby, knocking Martin to the ground.

In a moment there flashed before him all the sins he had ever committed. He saw again the stained-glass window in the Mansfeld church that had terrified him as a boy. It portrayed Jesus with a frowning face, sitting on a rainbow. On one side was a lily representing Jesus' blessing on the good. A flaming sword on the other side symbolized His anger against the wicked. There was no doubt in Martin's mind as he lay on the wet ground that stormy day. God was angry with him.

He remembered, too, the altarpiece, which depicted a ship sailing toward heaven with only priests and monks on board. The common people were drowning in the sea except for a few who grasped ropes thrown out by the holy men. Becoming a monk seemed the only way to salvation.

And so he cried out, "Lord, save me! Save me from this storm and I will become a monk!"

And there was no better monk than Martin Luther. He spent hours in fasting and prayer. He beat himself in penance for his sins. He refused blankets in winter to show remorse for his wicked ways. He had been taught that only by an adequate amount of suffering could forgiveness be his. Once, he confessed his sins to another priest for six hours straight before he ran out of wrongs he had committed, and still he could sense no forgiveness.

At last, Martin decided to make a pilgrimage to Rome. There he would climb "Pilate's staircase." This staircase, he believed, by some miraculous means, had been transported from Jerusalem to Rome, and great merit could be earned by climbing those steps.

So determined was Martin to get his sins forgiven that

he climbed each step on his knees, reciting his prayers on each step. He was midway up the stairs when he seemed to hear a voice that spoke like thunder, "The just shall live by faith!"

Martin had no doubt that it was God's voice. The truth of it shook his soul as the lightning had shaken the ground years before. He jumped to his feet and ran down the stairs and into the sunlight. For the first time in his life, Martin felt the peace of God's forgiveness.

Lord, I promise You that never again will I preach the doctrines and sayings of the popes, but will carefully study Your Word and preach it to the people. Your Word and Your Word only will be my rule of faith and practice! vowed Martin as he walked through the cobblestoned streets of Rome that day.

Twelve years later, on the night of October 31, 1517, Martin Luther climbed another set of steps, the ones leading to the great doors of the castle church in Wittenburg. In his hand was a roll of paper with ninety-five propositions against the doctrine of indulgences then being promoted by a priest named Tetzel and one Frederick of Saxony.

Tetzel sold certificates that assured people that their sins were forgiven and that they could go straight to heaven when they died. You could even buy these certificates for people who were already dead and were supposed to be suffering for their sins in purgatory. Tetzel had announced, "Once the money in the box rings, the soul from fiery purgatory wings."

Frederick of Saxony had more than 17,000 so-called holy objects that he kept in his house. There were such things as a piece of wood supposedly from the cross, a thorn said to be from the crown of Jesus, or a tooth purported to have belonged to one of the apostles. People could pay money to see these objects and thereby get thousands of years of release from purgatory.

Having found forgiveness through faith alone, Luther was determined to share the good news with the hundreds of worshipers during the festival of All Saints. He invited debate on the subject, promising to show people the truth from God's Word.

The posting of those ninety-five reasons has been called the beginning of the Protestant Reformation.

Epilogue

Between 1517 and 1520, Luther argued his case for the supremacy of Scripture and the priesthood of all believers, both in the pulpit and by his published treatises.

In 1520, a papal bull ordered Luther's recantation and the burning of all his works. He was brought to trial in Worms, where he made the famous pronouncement, "My conscience is captive to the Word of God . . . Here I stand, I can do no other."

Luther was then "kidnapped" by friends and protected in the castle of Wartburg under disguise as "George the Knight." While there, he began the translation of the New Testament from the Greek into the German language. It was published in 1522. His publication of the German Old Testament came in 1534.

While confined in Wartburg, Luther came to believe that he no longer needed to keep the vow of celibacy. He later married a former nun, Katherine of Bora, after helping her and other nuns escape from a convent. They had six children.

Born in 1483, Luther died in 1546 at the age of 64. He is known as the Father of the German Reformation and the founder of the Lutheran Church. Approximately 400,000,000 Protestants worldwide trace their spiritual roots to Martin Luther and his discovery of Romans 1:17 on "Pilate's staircase."

For other foundation can no man lay
than that is laid, which is Jesus Christ.

1 Corinthians 3:11

Revival's
Elect Lady

William Smith, provost of the University of Pennsylvania, founded a settlement upcountry in 1792. He named it Huntingdon, the name of the city and the county to this day. He did this to honor Selina, the Countess of Huntingdon, a Christian widow and philanthropist who had died in England the year before at the age of eighty-three.

Selina was a patron of the evangelical revival in eighteenth-century England led by John Wesley and George Whitefield. Widowed in 1746, she devoted her time, influence, and considerable fortune to the advancement of the cause and became known as the "elect lady" of the Methodist revival.

Three evenings each week, she invited the notable of

the land to her drawing rooms in London and arranged for John Wesley, Whitefield, and others to share the gospel with them. Princes and poets, actors and authors, sages and statesmen all were invited to enjoy her hospitality and heard the evangel. Great scoffers and the most dissolute of men accepted her invitations.

All who were considered distinguished or notable were among her guests. She took a movement spreading among the common and the poor of England and introduced it to courts and castles.

When clergymen of the established Church of England refused to allow evangelicals like Whitefield in their pulpits, she used her privileges as a countess to open "proprietary" chapels and appoint evangelical ministers to them. Selina eventually had thirty-six such chapels in places such as Brighton, Bath, Lewes, Tunbridge Wells, Hereford, Canterbury, Norwich, and Worcester.

In 1767, six theological students were expelled from Oxford University because of their Methodist leanings. She then established her own college in Wales to train evangelical ministers.

Lady Huntingdon supported George Whitefield in his missionary work in America and had a part in the founding of Dartmouth College and Princeton University. She supported missions in West Africa, the South Seas, and among the native Americans. She carefully controlled her household expenses so she could support her missions. By the time she died, she had spent her entire fortune.

What motivated this noblewoman to such exploits for the cross? How did she come to trust in Jesus? What was the secret that drove her to work with such zeal for the salvation of others?

One afternoon, nine-year-old Selina was walking with her sisters when they met a village funeral. It was the funeral of a child, a girl of nine, the same age as she. The reality of death suddenly hit her. She insisted on following the funeral to the grave site and came away in a very serious frame of mind.

From that day forward, Selina devoted herself to attending worship in the local chapel and to the reading of the Scriptures. She determined to find the assurance of happiness in the world to come.

As a young woman, she aspired after rectitude and was eager to possess every moral perfection. She grew rigidly just in all of her dealings and was inflexibly true to her word. She was strict in the observance of her duties in all the relationships of her life.

But somehow Selina's attempts at righteousness did not satisfy. Wealth, beauty, and popularity were hers; but they were not enough. She felt that her heart was evil and that her sins brought her under the condemnation of God.

Selina married the Earl of Huntingdon. She became close friends with his two sisters, Lady Betty and Lady Margaret Hastings. Both were deeply religious. By this time, both Wesley and Whitefield were preaching in the open air—in fields, in lanes, and on village greens. Both the Lady Margaret and the Lady Betty had been to hear them.

When Selina fell dangerously ill, she thought again of her sinful state and her lack of assurance of eternal life. Sister-in-law Lady Margaret sat by her bedside and shared her own experience. "Since I have trusted in Jesus for life and salvation I have been as happy as an angel," she said.

As soon as Selina was well enough to read, she called for a Bible. She opened to 1 Corinthians, her favorite book. She read on until she came to 3:11, "For other foundation can no man lay than that is laid, which is Jesus Christ."

The words of Lady Margaret returned, "Since I have trusted in Jesus for life and salvation I have been as happy as an angel." It seemed that scales fell from Selina's eyes, and she recognized the significance of this powerful passage, "Other foundation can no man lay than that is laid, which is Jesus Christ."

Renouncing every other hope, Selina cast herself wholly upon Christ for life and salvation. From her bed, she lifted up her heart to her Saviour. Suddenly, all fear and distress fled. For the first time in her life, her heart was filled with joy and peace.

She determined thenceforth to give herself a living sacrifice to Jesus, who gave her such beautiful assurance.

Epilogue

Due to a lawsuit, she had to register her chapels as dissenting meeting houses in 1779. They became part of what was known as the Countess of Huntingdon Connexion, although she continued a devout Anglican. The college she had founded in Wales was moved to Cambridge in 1904.

In tribute to her, Wesley once said, "I wish I had a Countess of Huntingdon in every parish of the kingdom." When Lady Charlotte Edwin mocked Selina, the crown prince rebuked her saying, "I would be pleased on my deathbed to touch the Countess of Huntingdon's mantle."

*N*ow if any man build upon this foundation
gold, silver, precious stones, wood, hay, stubble;
every man's work shall be made manifest;
for the day shall declare it,
because it shall be revealed by fire;
and the fire shall try every man's work of what sort it is.
If any man's work abide which he hath built thereupon,
he shall receive a reward.

1 Corinthians 3:12-14

A Voice in the Wind

It was a gray, cloudy Sunday in Belfast, Ireland. The Carmichael family was walking home from a fashionable church when they passed an old woman in rags carrying a heavy bundle.

"Look at that poor woman!" seventeen-year-old Amy exclaimed. "She needs help!" Running to her side, she offered, "Here, let me help you."

Immediately her two brothers were at her side, lifting down the heavy package from the woman's back. One brother shouldered the bundle while Amy and the other brother took hold of the woman's feeble arms and steadied her as she walked.

Respectable church members frowned as they saw the Carmichaels helping the disheveled old woman.

"It was a horrid moment," Amy admitted afterward. "We were only two boys and a girl, and not at all exalted Christians. We hated doing it. Crimson all over (at least we felt crimson, soul and body of us), we plodded on, a wet wind blowing us about, and blowing, too, the rags of the poor old woman, till she seemed like a bundle of feathers, and we unhappily mixed up with them."

At that moment, the words of 1 Corinthians 3:12-14 came clearly to Amy's mind, "Gold, silver, precious stones, wood, hay, stubble; every man's work shall be made manifest; for the day shall declare it, because it shall be revealed by fire; and the fire shall try every man's work of what sort it is."

Amy heard the words so distinctly that she turned to see who had spoken but saw nobody, only the muddy street, people walking home from church, and the village fountain bubbling in the gray drizzle.

Amy said nothing of her experience at the time but later wrote, "I knew that something had happened that had changed life's values. Nothing could ever matter again but the things that were eternal."

Shortly after that, Amy began holding children's meetings at her home, then went to work at the Belfast City Mission, teaching a boy's class and later a class for poor girls who worked in her father's mills.

Coming from a wealthy home, Amy enjoyed pretty clothes as much as any girl of privilege. However, after this encounter with God's Word, Amy felt other things were more important.

On one occasion, Amy's mother took her shopping in Belfast for a new evening dress. The shopkeeper brought out his loveliest silks and satins. As Amy looked at the beautiful cloth, she thought, *What are parties and fine clothes in the light of eternity?*

"Mother, I can't do this," Amy whispered. "I don't want a new evening dress. I have plenty of clothes already. Other things are now more important to me."

Embarrassed, her mother made some excuse to the shopkeeper, and they walked out. She couldn't understand what had happened to her vivacious daughter who had used to so love shopping for fine velvets and silks.

Amy's life was never the same after that brief encounter with God's Word at the village fountain. Ever after, she looked at everything through the lens of eternity. As each decision in life came up, she would ask herself, "In the light of eternity, what difference will this make?"

Epilogue

Amy Carmichael spent fifty-five years as a missionary in South India, beginning in 1895. In Tinnevelly, she began rescuing young temple prostitutes, later founding Dohnavur Fellowship to care for these girls as well as orphaned children. No accurate record was kept, but it is estimated that several thousand children were rescued from temple prostitution. At times, there were as many as 800 children being cared for in three homes.

In 1919, Amy was scheduled to receive a medal from

the governor of Madras for her work for the people of India. She nearly refused it. She said, "It troubles me to have an experience so different from His who was despised and rejected—not kindly honored."

Before she died at her post in 1951, Amy had written thirty-eight books of her experiences in India, as well as poetry and devotional thoughts that have inspired thousands of Christians during the last century.

About the influence of Amy Carmichael on her life, Elisabeth Elliot wrote, "When I was fourteen years old, a student in boarding school, I first heard of Amy Carmichael. The headmistress of the school often quoted her writings and told of her amazing work in India for the rescue of little children in moral danger. No other single individual has had a more powerful influence on my own life and writing than Amy Carmichael. No one else put the missionary call more clearly."

Margaret Bendroth would agree. She writes in *More Than Conquerors*, "Amy Carmichael's life . . . is an unparalleled example of spiritual passion. . . . Nothing was more precious than her calling, and all her life she followed a soul-uprooting quest for pure knowledge of God. . . . Her fiery singleness of purpose re-ignites the power of the simple gospel."

In her book *Guardians of the Great Commission*, Ruth Tucker says, "Amy Carmichael, through her many years of service in India and her numerous books, is one of the most widely known missionaries of the twentieth century."

Don't be vague
but grasp firmly what you know
to be the will of the Lord.
Ephesians 5:17 (Phillips)

Saved From Suicide

Joyce stared at the medicine cabinet. Slowly she opened the door, took out an unopened packet of razor blades, and removed the wrapper. *Soon I'll be free from this horrid world forever,* Joyce thought as she carefully drew one blade out of the package. She lowered the blade to her wrist. At that precise moment, the shrill ring of the phone cut through the heavy stillness.

Razor blade poised she counted the rings. *Seven, eight, nine . . . Won't it ever stop? . . . ten, eleven, twelve . . . Hang up! I'm not going to answer! . . . thirteen, fourteen . . . What could be so important?*

Dropping the razor blade, Joyce ran to the bedroom, jerked the receiver off the hook, and shouted, "Hello!"

"Hello, Joyce, this is Chuck Leviton," he spoke gently. "I don't know what you're doing right now, but stop whatever it is and listen to me." *Oh no! Not a minister! I don't need you nor your Bible*, Joyce thought. She had met Chuck months before at a Youth for Christ rally in Phoenix. Why was he calling now?

Chuck began reading from Ephesians, "Don't be vague but grasp firmly what you know to be the will of the Lord." He read on, but Joyce's mind was fixed on that one phrase, "firmly grasp what you KNOW to be the will of the Lord." *Oh, God, what is your will for me?*

After Chuck hung up, Joyce returned to the bathroom and looked at herself in the mirror. Although she was only twenty-five years old, a haggard old woman with vacant eyes stared back at her. Suddenly, the timing of that phone call hit her. *God must have some reason for me to live!*

Into her mind popped a verse she had once memorized, "The Son of man is come to seek and to save that which was lost." *That's me!* Joyce thought. *I'm lost as a wife, mother, cook, and a human being. Could it be that God cares about me?*

Another verse came unbidden to her mind, "If we confess our sins, he is faithful and just to forgive us our sins, and to cleanse us from all unrighteousness."

Joyce ran to the living room and knelt in front of a green wingbacked chair. It seemed her whole sordid life passed before her eyes in the next few seconds. From deep within she cried out, "My God, my God, forgive me! Me, Lord, me!"

Tears flowed down her cheeks as she continued to kneel, waiting for God to do something. Slowly a sense of His presence and His unconditional, forgiving love flooded her whole being.

About that moment, Joyce writes, "What joy, what incredible joy. The silent, yet expectant peace that followed in the next few moments was breath-taking. Nothing seemed to move, and I was suspended on the very wings of angels."

Epilogue

Joyce Landorf Heatherly went on to become the author of more than twenty books such as *His Stubborn Love*, *Irregular People*, *Silent September*, *Balcony People*, and *Unworld People*.

This is a faithful saying,
and worthy of all acceptation,
that Christ Jesus came into the world to save sinners;
of whom I am chief.

1 Timothy 1:15

A Fire in His Heart

During the short five-year reign of Mary Tudor, 300 persons were put to death for their belief that they could come directly to God through Jesus without the mediation of saints and priests. Thus, that queen has been remembered for 400 years as "Bloody Mary."

Most of the martyrs were simple working men who had learned to read the Bible and follow its precepts in the previous reign of her brother, Edward VI.

But others thought justice could be better served by bringing some of the Protestant leaders, who had taught these people, to martyrdom. Thus in September 1553, Bishops Thomas Cranmer, Nicholas Ridley, and Hugh Latimer were brought from the Queen's prison in the Tower of London to Oxford to be examined for their heresies. They refused to accept the church's teaching on the Mass and were excommunicated and condemned to death.

Latimer was now a frail eighty years of age with a failing memory. But he refused to recant and stood firm for his faith and rigidly rejected the idea that the Mass was a valid sacrifice for sin.

The Martyrs Memorial in the university city of Oxford hallows the spot where Hugh Latimer and Nicholas Ridley were burned at the stake on October 6, 1555.

They knelt together and prayed before the pyre. Then they were fastened by chains to an iron post, and each had a bag of gunpowder hung around his neck, to lessen his pain when it exploded. The fires were then lighted.

Latimer encouraged Ridley with the words, "Be of good comfort, Master Ridley, and play the man. We shall this day light such a candle, by God's grace, in England, as I trust shall never be put out!"

The eighty-year-old Latimer did not suffer long. As the faggots (sticks) were heaped around him and everything was ready, he raised his eyes to heaven. In an instant, the gunpowder exploded, and his feeble frame succumbed.

In his earlier days, Latimer, as a priest of the Roman faith, preached very fervently against any changes in the time-hallowed religious practices of the day. His early beliefs were entirely orthodox. His bachelor of divinity oration at Cambridge was an attack on the teachings of Luther.

Thirty years before the martyr's fire was lighted at Oxford, a powerful passage of Scripture lighted another fire in Latimer's heart. It was the fire of faith in Jesus as his one true Mediator. It was a conversion as sudden and unexpected as that of Paul on the Damascus road. He claimed it came through a contact with Thomas Bilney.

"Little Bilney," as he was called, came to faith in Christ through reading Erasmus's New Testament in Latin at Cambridge. He preached against the worship of saints, ceremonies, and pilgrimages for the forgiveness of sin. He died for his faith under Cardinal Wolsey in 1531— one of the first Protestant martyrs in England.

As he listened to Latimer preaching at Cambridge, Bilney prayed that God would use him to bring enlightenment to that great man. When Latimer descended from the pulpit, Bilney followed him to his room and requested, "I pray thee, Father Latimer, may I confess my soul to thee?"

Latimer beckoned him to the adjoining room. Bilney, on his knees, shared with Latimer the aching hunger of his life. He said, "My soul was sick and I longed for peace, but nowhere could I find it. I went to the priests and they appointed me penances and pilgrimages; yet by these things my poor sick soul was nothing profited. They pointed me to broken cisterns that held no water and only mocked my thirst!" He confessed how he bore the burden of his sins until his soul was crushed by the load.

Then Bilney met Erasmus and purchased the Scriptures. In them he discovered 1 Timothy 1:15. With tears in his eyes, he told Latimer, "There it stood, the very word I wanted. It seemed to be written in letters of light . . . and now being justified by faith, I have peace with God through our Lord Jesus Christ."

An astounding thing happened. Overwhelmed by that testimony, Latimer rose and knelt beside Bilney. He, too, had for years experienced the same awful hunger and insatiable thirst. He needed what Bilney had found. "Show me that text," Latimer begged. "I need the comfort of those words."

Bilney drew from his pocket his New Testament and showed the powerful passage to Latimer, "Christ Jesus came into the world to save sinners; of whom I am chief."

Latimer believed and a fire was lighted in his soul that nothing could extinguish.

Epilogue

Latimer, certified by the University at Oxford, was authorized to preach in any church in England. He preached before both Henry VIII and his son Edward VII and was an advocate for the Reformation in both their reigns.

He served as the Bishop of Worcester for five years but was forced to resign when he refused to sign the Six Articles that were introduced to prevent the spread of Protestant doctrines.

Latimer's sermons attracted large crowds and were appreciated by the common people for their directness and simplicity. His emphasis was practical rather than theological.

Latimer preached in the open air to 6,000 people at a time. Parish records show that church benches had to be repaired after his sermons because of the crowds.

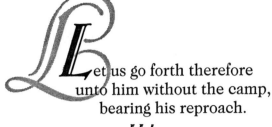

Let us go forth therefore
unto him without the camp,
bearing his reproach.

Hebrews 13:13

The Father of Modern Missions

Two hundred years ago, a boy named Billy played in a country lane in England. He saw a bird's nest in a chestnut tree and climbed the tree to get the nest. He fell down. He climbed a second time. And fell. He climbed a third time. This time, his fall broke a leg.

A few weeks later, his mother left him in the kitchen for an hour while she ran some errands. The leg was still bandaged. "Billy," she said, "be careful while I'm gone."

When she returned, he was sitting on his chair, flushed, excited, with the bird's nest on his knees. "Hurrah, Mother! I've done it at last! Here it is. Look!"

"You don't mean to tell me you climbed that tree again!"

"I couldn't help it, Mother. You see, if I begin a thing, I must go through with it."

That statement helps me understand how when that boy became a man, he mastered a dozen languages including Greek, Hebrew, and Latin. He translated the Bible into Sanskrit, Bengali, Marathi, and three other languages. He established a Christian college near Calcutta. He inspired the formation of several hundred missionary societies and became known as "the father of modern missions."

The family was poor. When William was fourteen, his father apprenticed him to a cobbler to learn the shoemaker's trade. Using scraps of leather, he fashioned himself a world map and traced the voyages of Captain Cook.

William Carey's father and grandfather had both taught the village school. Books were available to him. He learned to read the Bible and to attend the Church of England services regularly. His father taught him to fear God and honor the king.

Carey was proud to be a member of the established church. He had little sympathy for nonconformists who dissented. But over time, he learned to appreciate the friendship of John Warr, one of the dissenters.

Carey and Warr talked for hours about work, sports, and girls. However, discussions on religion were quite heated.

Carey thought of dissenters as enemies to the security of Britain. In the previous century, the Puritans under Cromwell had executed King Charles I. Therefore, Carey labeled the dissenters as regicides, religious fanatics, and republicans. Did they not realize that the greatness of Britain depended on the monarchy and the established church? Already there was a stirring among the colonists in America against the king. Did not the future greatness of the empire depend on loyalty to the crown?

Warr did not argue with Carey but witnessed to him about his need to repent of his sins and accept Jesus as his Saviour.

Carey vigorously protested, "I was baptized as an infant, am a member of the church, and therefore I am already a Christian. I have no need to repent."

But one day in collecting a bill for his master, Carey exchanged a counterfeit shilling, received as a tip, and gave that to his master instead. He worried greatly about the discovery of his dishonesty. He even prayed that he would not be found out! But he was.

The legal penalty for the theft of a shilling was death or transportation to the colonies in America. However, his master didn't press charges. Carey felt ashamed.

Again Warr talked about the power of Jesus to forgive, cleanse, and give victory over sin. However, Carey thought, *I will make myself better through greater zeal in attending prayer meeting and church.* For some time, he refused to admit that he couldn't make himself a better man, even though he knew he was unable to clean his tongue from lying, swearing, and impurity. Finally, he realized the need for something more than a form of religion and began attending the dissenter's chapel with John Warr.

One night, a novice at preaching pleaded for a whole-hearted surrender to Christ, quoting the words of Hebrews 13:13, "Let us go forth therefore unto him without the camp, bearing his reproach."

God spoke powerfully to Carey through that scripture. He went through a terrible struggle. At last he made his decision to surrender all to Jesus. For him, that included joining the dissenters whom he had so thoroughly despised, thus going "without the camp" of the established church.

Epilogue

Carey became a Baptist pastor. Convinced that Christians should take the gospel to the non-Christian world, he pleaded with fellow ministers to establish a missionary society. On October 2, 1792, they formed the Baptist Missionary Society. He became their first missionary, sailing to India in 1793.

Carey inspired the formation of the London Missionary Society, the Church Missionary Society, the American Board of Commissioners for Foreign Missions, the British Methodist Missionary Society, the American Baptist Missionary Union, and numerous others.

By 1900, there were more than 300 such societies. The efforts of the missionary societies made the nineteenth century the "Great Century" of modern missions.

In 1800, only eighteen percent of the world's population professed faith in Christ. By 1900, it had risen to 30 percent.

In 1800, only one in a hundred believers were in what is called the South—Asia, Latin America, Africa, the South Pacific, and the Caribbean. Ninety-nine percent of believers were in the North—Europe, North America, Australia, and New Zealand. By 1995, two of every three believers were in the South and only one in three in the North. Carey's vision had globalized Protestant Christianity.

People Index

Bibliographical References

Joshua 24:15: A Man of Courage

Douglas, J. D., and Philip W. Comfort, eds., *Who's Who in Christian History*. Wheaton, Ill.: Tyndale House Publishers, Inc., 1992. Pages 291, 292.
Encylopedia Britannica. Chicago, Ill.: William Benton, 1965. Volume 10, page 915.
Fisk, Samuel. *40 Fascinating Conversion Stories*. Grand Rapids, Mich.: Kregel Publications, 1993. Pages 55-58.
Kerr, Hugh T. and John M. Mulder. *Famous Conversions*. Grand Rapids, Mich.: William B. Eerdmans Publishing Company, 1983. Pages 164-167.
Tucker, Ruth. *From Jerusalem to Irian Jaya*. Grand Rapids, Mich.: Zondervan Pub. House, 1983. Pages 329-332.
Watts, Dorothy Eaton. *This Is The Day*. Hagerstown, Md.: Review and Herald Publishing Assoc., 1982. Page 119.
World Book Encyclopedia. Chicago, Ill.: Field Enterprises Educational Corporation, 1973. Volume 8, page 382.

1 Kings 18:39: God's Last Chance

Anders, Isabel. *Standing on High Places*. Wheaton, Ill.: Tyndale House Publishers, Inc., 1994. Pages 9-15.
Watts, Dorothy Eaton. *Pursuing His Presence*. Hagerstown, Md.: Review and Herald Pub. Assoc., 1996. Pages 13-23.

Psalm 19:9: Gettysburg Surrender

McPherson, James M. *Battle Cry of Freedom*. New York: Oxford University Press, 1988. Pages 181, 182, 312, 536-545.

Sears, Stephen W. *Landscape Turned Red.* New York: Warner Books, 1983. Pages 122-127.

Van Doren, Charles A. *A History of Knowledge.* New York: Ballantine Books, 1992. Pages 275-278.

Woodbridge, John, ed. *More Than Conquerors.* Chicago, Ill.: Moody Press, 1992. Pages 14-21.

World Book Encyclopedia. Toronto: Field Enterprises Educational Corp., 1973. Volume 12, Pages 275-284.

Psalm 37:3, 4: The Watergate Scandal

Colson, Charles W. *Born Again.* New York: Bantam Books, 1977. Page 406.

Kerr, Hugh T. and John M. Mulder, eds. *Famous Conversions.* Grand Rapids, Mich.: William B. Eerdmans Publishing, 1983. Pages 106, 107.

Shepard, Stephen B., ed. *Business Week.* New York: McGraw-Hill Companies, 27 March 1955. Pages 106, 107.

Woodbridge, John D., ed. *More Than Conquerors.* Chicago, Ill.: Moody Press, 1992. Pages 265-269.

Psalm 51:10: Letter from an Old Friend

Boreham, F. W. *Life Verses.* Grand Rapids, Mich.: Kregel Publications, 1994. Volume 4, pages 9-20.

Douglas, J. D. and Philip W. Comfort, eds. *Who's Who in Christian History.* Wheaton, Ill.: Tyndale House Publishers, 1992. Page 266.

Encyclopedia Britannica. Chicago, Ill,: William Benton, 1965. Volume 7, Page 776; Volume 16, Page 46.

Fisk, Samuel. *More Fascinating Conversion Stories.* Grand Rapids, Mich.: Kregel Publications, 1994. Page 47-52.

Latourette, Kenneth S. *A History of the Expansion of Christianity.* Grand Rapids, Mich.: Zondervan Publishing House, 1943. Volume 5, Pages 102, 103, 355.

Proverbs 8:35: Running From God

Blackburn, Joyce. *Roads to Reality.* Old Tappan, N.J.: Fleming H. Revell

Co., 1979. Pages 23-29.

Price, Eugenia. *Inside One Author's Heart.* New York: Doubleday, 1992.

Woodbridge, John, ed. *More Than Conquerors.* Chicago, Ill.: Moody Press, 1992. Pages 131-133.

Proverbs 16:32: Behind the Bathroom Door

Carson, Ben, M.D. with Cecil Murphey. *Gifted Hands.* Hagerstown, Md.: Review and Herald Pub. Assoc., 1990. Page 54-60.

Carson, Benjamin S., M.D. "Standing on God's Promise." *Guideposts.* June 1988. Pages 6-9.

Jackson-Hall, Barbara. "Dr. Ben Carson, The Lord Guided His Hands." *Message.* March/April 1988. Pages 2-21.

Watts, Dorothy Eaton. *Friends for Keeps.* Hagerstown, Md.: Review and Herald Pub. Assoc., 1995. Page 17.

Isaiah 11:9: Now God Speaks Our Language!

Fisk, Samuel. *40 Fascinating Conversion Stories.* Grand Rapids, Mich.: Kregel Publications, 1993. Pages 155-158.

Shibley, David, and Naomi Shibley. *The Smoke of A Thousand Villages.* Nashville, Tenn.: Thomas Nelson Publishers, 1989. Pages 105-111.

Tucker Ruth A. *From Jerusalem to Irian Jaya.* Grand Rapids, Mich.: Zondervan, 1983. Pages 351-357.

Woodbridge, John D., ed. *Ambassadors for Christ.* Chicago, Ill.: Moody Press, 1994. Pages 118-126.

Isaiah 45:22: Finding God in a Snowstorm

Calkins, Harold L. *Master Preachers.* Hagerstown, Md.: Review and Herald Publishing Association, 1960. Pages 45-48.

Cowart, John W. *People Whose Faith Got Them Into Trouble.* Downers Grove, Ill.: InterVarsity Press, 1990. Pages 1-108.

Fisk Samuel. *40 Fascinating Conversion Stories.* Grand Rapids, Mich.: Kregel Publications, 1993. Pages 135-138.

Watts, Dorothy Eaton. *This Is The Day.* Hagerstown. Md.: Review and Herald Pub. Assoc., 1982. Page 92.

POWERFUL PASSAGES

Isaiah 53:6: The Unanswered Question

Gartenhaus, Jacob. *Famous Hebrew Christians.* Chattanooga, Tenn.: International Board of Jewish Missions, Inc., 1979. Pages 83-90.

Watts, Dorothy Eaton. *Friends for Keeps.* Hagerstown, Md.: Review and Herald Pub. Assoc., 1995.

Jeremiah 29:12, 13: It's This Week or Never!

Douglas, J. D. and Philip W. Comfort, eds. *Who's Who in Christian History.* Wheaton, Ill.: Tyndale House Publishers, Inc., 1992. Pages 247, 248.

Kerr, Hugh T. and John M. Mulder, eds. *Famous Conversions.* Grand Rapids, Mich.: William B. Eerdmans, 1983. Pages 3-13.

Wessel, Helen, ed. *The Autobiography of Charles G. Finney.* Minneapolis, Minn.: Bethany House Publishers, 1977. Pages 8-25.

Matthew 2:2: The Greatest Since Paul

Douglas, J. D. and Philip W. Comfort, eds. *Who's Who in Christian History.* Wheaton, Ill.: Tyndale House Publishers, Inc., 1992. Pages 386, 387.

Fisk, Samuel. *More Fascinating Conversion Stories.* Grand Rapids, Mich.: Kregel Publications, 1994. Pages 63-67.

Watts, Dorothy Eaton. *Stepping Stones.* Hagerstown, Md.: Review and Herald Pub. Assoc., 1987. Page 349.

Woodbridge, John D. ed. *Ambassadors for Christ.* Chicago, Ill.: Moody Press, 1994. Pages 30-35.

Matthew 5:3 - 11: Chance Meeting On A Train

Douglas, J. D. and Philip W. Comfort, eds. *Who's Who in Christian History.* Wheaton, Ill.: Tyndale House Publishers, Inc., 1992. Page 674.

Encylopedia Britannica. Chicago, Ill.: William Benton, 1965. Volume 5, page 25.

Fisk, Samuel. *More Fascinating Conversion Stories.* Grand Rapids, Mich.: Kregel Publications, 1994. Pages 155-158.

Bibliographical References

Matthew 5:4: A Scrap of Paper

Gartenhaus, Jacob. *Famous Hebrew Christians.* Chattanooga, Tenn.: International Board of Jewish Missions, Inc., 1979. Pages 99-104.

Encylopedia Britannica. Chicago, Ill.: Encyclopedia Britannica, Inc., 1965. Volume 11, page 452.

Matthew 7:24: God Speaks in Hollywood

Blackburn, Joyce. *Roads to Reality.* Old Tappan, N.J.: Fleming H. Revell Co., 1978. Pages 16-22.

Rogers, Dale Evans. *In the Hands of the Potter.* Nashville, Tenn.: Thomas Nelson Publishers, 1994. Pages 1-212.

Matthew 25:36, 37: The Unexpected Guest

Brand, Paul, Dr. and Philip Yancey. *The Gift Nobody Wants.* Grand Rapids, Mich.: HarperCollins, 1995. Pages 105, 106.

Spangler, Ann and Charles Turner, eds. *Meet the Men and Women We Call Heroes.* Ann Arbor, Mich.: Servant Publications, 1985. Pages 203-221.

Watts, Dorothy Eaton. *Stepping Stones.* Hagerstown, Md.: Review and Herald Pub. Assoc., 1987. Page 370.

Wilson, Dorothy Clarke. *Twelve Who Cared.* Toronto: Hodder & Stoughton, 1977. Pages 120-123.

Mark 8:35: The Price of Happiness

World Book Encyclopedia. Chicago, Ill.: Field Enterprises Educational Corporation, 1973. Volume 17, page 161.

Douglas, J. D. and Philip W. Comfort, eds. *Who's Who in Christian History.* Wheaton, Ill.: Tyndale House Publishers, Inc., 1992. Pages 614, 615.

Kerr, Hugh T. and John M. Mulder, eds. *Famous Conversions: The Christian Experience.* Grand Rapids, Mich.: William B. Eerdmans, 1983. Pages 189-194.

Tucker, Ruth A. *From Jerusalem to Irian Jaya.* Grand Rapids, Mich.: Zondervan Publishing House, 1983. Page 328.

Mark 8:36, 37: Street Corner Invitation

Boreham, F. W. *Life Verses.* Grand Rapids, Mich.: Kregel Publications, 1994. Volume 3, pages 189-199.

Douglas, J. D. and Philip W. Comfort, eds. *Who's Who In Christian History.* Wheaton, Ill.: TyndaleHouse Publishers, Inc., 1992. page 725.

Howell, Clifford G. *The Advance Guard of Missions.* Boise, Idaho: Pacific Press Pub. Assoc., 1912. Pages 248-257.

Mark 12:34: Not Far From the Kingdom

Boreham, F. W. *Life Verses.* Grand Rapids, Mich.: Kregel Publications, 1994. Volume 1, pages 198-209.

Douglas, J. D. and P. W.Comfort, eds. *Who's Who in Christian History.* Wheaton, Ill.: Tyndale House Publishers, 1992. Pages 709-712.

Encyclopedia Britannica. Chicago, Ill.: Wm. Benton, 1965. Volume 23, pages 516-518.

Fisk, Samuel. *More Fascinating Conversion Stories.* Grand Rapids, Mich.: Kregel Publications, 1994. Pages 173-176.

Kerry, Hugh T. and John M. Mulder. *Famous Conversions.* Grand Rapids, Mich.: Eerdmans, 1983. Pages 54-61.

Luke 15:20: A Voice in the Slums

Deen, Edith. *Great Women of the Christian Faith.* Westwood, N. J.: Barbour and Company, Inc., 1959. Pages 218-226.

Douglas, J. D. and Philip W. Comfort, eds. *Who's Who in Christian History.* Wheaton: Ill.: Tyndale House Publishers, Inc., 1992. Pages 93, 94.

Encyclopaedia Britannica. Chicago, Ill.: William Benton, Publisher, 1965. Volume 3, page 947.

Sotnak, Lewann. *Their Light Still Shines.* Minneapolis, Minn.: Augsburg Fortress, 1993. Pages 60-65.

Tucker, Ruth A. and Walter L. Liefeld. *Daughters of the Church.* Grand Rapids, Mich.: Zondervan Publishing House, 1987. Page 264-267.

Luke 15:20: Amazing Grace

Boreham, F. W. *Life Verses.* Grand Rapids, Mich.: Kregel Publications,

1994. Volume 1, pages 222-234.

Douglas, J. D. and P. W.Comfort, eds. *Who's Who in Christian History*. Wheaton, Ill.: Tyndale House Publishers, 1992. Page 506.

Encyclopedia Britannica. Chicago, Ill.: William Benton, 1965. Volume 16, Page 420.

Fisk, Samuel. *40 Fascinating Conversion Stories*. Grand Rapids, Mich.: Kregel Publications, 1993. Pages 105-110.

Kerr, Hugh T. and John M. Mulder. *Famous Conversions*. Grand Rapids, Mich.: Eerdmans, 1983. Pages 87-91.

Styles, Jim. *Let's Talk About Olney's Amazing Curate*. Newport Pagnell, U.K.: A. C. Todd, 1983. Page 22.

World Book Encyclopedia. Toronto: Field Enterprises Educational Corporation, 1973. Volume 12, page 307.

Luke 18:13: The Hunchback of Westminster Abbey

Boreham, F. W. *Life Verses*. Grand Rapids, Mich.: Kregel Publications, 1994. Volume 1, pages 185-187.

Douglas, J. D. and P. W. Comfort, eds. *Who's Who in Christian History*. Wheaton, Ill.: Tyndale House Publishers, 1992. Page 719.

Encyclopedia Britannica. Chicago, Ill.: William Benton, 1965. Volume 23, Page 596.

Fisk, Samuel. *40 Fascinating Conversion Stories*. Grand Rapids, Mich.: Kregel Publications, 1993. Pages 177-182.

Patten, John A. *These Remarkable Men*. London: Lutterworth Press, 1945. Pages 11-45.

Pollock, John. *Wilberforce*. Belleville, Mich.: Lion Publishing Corp., 1977. Page 368.

Turner, Charles, ed. *Chosen Vessels*. Ann Arbor, Mich.: Servant Publications, 1985. Pages 41-72.

Woodbridge, John, ed. *More Than Conquerors*. Chicago, Ill.: Moody Press, 1992. Pages 240-244.

Luke 23:34: A Gentleman in Prison

Boreham, F. W. *Life Verses*. Grand Rapids, Mich.: Kregel Publications, 1994. Volume 4, Pages 168-180.

POWERFUL PASSAGES

John 1:1: Discovery in a Barn

Barrett, Eric C. and David Fisher, eds. *Scientists Who Believe.* Chicago, Ill.: Moody Press, 1984. Pages 1-9.

John 4:7: Hindu Woman at the Well

Anonymous. *Heroes of the Cross, Series II.* London: Marshall, Morgan, and Scott, Ltd., 1933. Pages 5-32.

Deen, Edith. *Great Women of the Christian Faith.* Westwood, N.J.: Barbour and Co., Inc., 1959. Pages 258-268.

McElrath, William N. *Bold Bearers of His Name.* Nashville, Tenn.: Broadman Press, 1987. Pages 24-31.

Tucker, Ruth A. and Walter L. Liefeld. *Daughters of the Church.* Grand Rapids, Mich.: Zondervan Publishing House, 1987. Pages 344-347.

Woodbridge, John D., ed. *Ambassadors for Christ.* Chicago, Ill.: Moody Press, 1994. Pages 167-173.

John 5:24: Born Walking

Fisk, Samuel. *40 Fascinating Conversion Stories.* Grand Rapids, Mich.: Kregel Publications, 1993. Pages 163-165.

Shibley, David and Naomi Shibley. *The Smoke of a Thousand Villages.* Nashville, Tenn.: Thomas Nelson Publishers, 1989. Pages 112-115.

Woodbridge, John, ed. *More Than Conquerors.* Chicago, Ill.: Moody Press, 1992. Pages 165-168.

John 5:39: The Barefoot Seeker

Watts, Dorothy Eaton. *This Is The Day.* Hagerstown, Md.: Review and Herald Pub. Assoc., 1982. Page 74.

John 6:37: A Musty Old Book

Douglas, J. D. and P. W. Comfort, eds. *Who's Who in Christian History.* Wheaton, Ill.: Tyndale House Publishers, 1992. Page 625.

Fisk, Samuel. *40 Fascinating Conversion Stories.* Grand Rapids, Mich.: Kregel Publications, 1993. Pages 127-130.

Tucker, Ruth A. *From Jerusalem to Irian Jaya.* Grand Rapids, Mich.: Zondervan, 1983. Pages 290-295.

John 11:26: An Agnostic Finds Christ

Johnson, A. Wetherell. *Created for Commitment.* Wheaton, Ill.: Tyndale House Pub., Inc., 1982. Pages 40-43.
Woodbridge, John, ed. *More Than Conquerors.* Chicago, Ill.: Moody Bible Institute, 1992. Pages 79-83.

John 17:25: Night of Fire

Boreham, F. W. *Life Verses.* Grand Rapids, Mich.: Kregel Publications, 1994. Volume 4, pages 203-214.
Douglas, J. D. and P. W. Comfort, eds. *Who's Who In Christian History.* Wheaton, Ill.: Tyndale House Publishers, 1992. Pages 531, 532.
Durant, Will and Ariel Durant. *The Reformation.* New York: Simon & Schuster, 1957. Pages 55-67.
Encyclopedia Britannica. Chicago, Ill.: William Benton, 1965. Volume 17, page 351.
Kerr, Hugh T. and John M. Mulder. *Famous Conversions.* Grand Rapids, Mich.: Eerdmans, 1983. Pages 36-40.
Spangler, Ann and Charles Turner, eds. *Meet the Men and Women We Call Heroes.* Ann Arbor, Mich.: Servant Publications, 1985. Pages 323-332.
World Book Encyclopedia. Toronto: Field Enterprises Educational Corporation, 1973. Volume 2, page 84; Volume 9, page 410; Volume 10, page 242; Volume 15, pages 166, 684.

John 18:26: The Scottish Sword-bearer

Boreham, F. W. *Life Verses.* Grand Rapids, Mich.: Kregel Publications, 1994. Volume 1, pages 110-119.
Douglas, J. D. and P. W. Comfort, eds. *Who's Who in Christian History.* Wheaton, Ill.: Tyndale House Publishers, 1992. Pages 402-404.
Durant, Will and Ariel Durant. *The Reformation.* New York: Simon & Schuster, 1957. Pages 607-615.
Encyclopedia Britannica. Chicago, Ill,: William Benton, 1965. Volume

13, pages 433-436.

Lamont, Stewart. *The Swordbearer.* London: Hodder and Stoughton, 1991.

World Book Encyclopedia. Toronto: Field Enterprises Educational Corporation, 1973. Volume 11, Page 285.

John 19:28: Thirsty No More

Douglas, J. D. and P. W. Comfort, eds. *Who's Who in Christian History.* Wheaton, Ill.: Tyndale House Publishers, 1992. Pages 716, 717.

Encyclopedia Britannica. Chicago, Ill.: William Benton, 1965. Volume 23, Page 576.

Kerr, Hugh T. and John M. Mulder. *Famous Conversions.* Grand Rapids, Mich.: Eerdmans, 1983. Pages 61-66.

World Book Encyclopedia. Toronto: Field Enterprises Educational Corporation, 1973. Volume 2, page 84; Volume 21, page 244.

John 19:30: Forgiveness in a Hayloft

Douglas, J. D. and P. W. Comfort, eds. *Who's Who in Christian History.* Wheaton, Ill.: Tyndale House Publishers, 1992. Pages 657-659.

Howell, Clifford G. *The Advance Guard of Missions.* Boise, Idaho: Pacific Press Pub. Assoc., 1912. Pages 299-323.

Shibley, David and Naomi Shibley. *The Smoke of a Thousand Villages.* Nashville, Tenn.: Thomas Nelson Publishers, 1989. Pages 99-104.

Tucker, Ruth A. *From Jerusalem to Irian Jaya.* Grand Rapids, Mich.: Zondervan, 1983. Pages 173-188.

Woodbridge, John D., ed. *Ambassadors for Christ.* Chicago, Ill.: Moody Press, 1994. Pages 157-162.

Woodbridge, John, ed. *More Than Conquerors.* Chicago, Ill.: Moody Bible Institute, 1992. Pages 50-55.

Acts 16:19-34: How The Burglar Got Caught

Moody, D. L. Moody. "A Change of Heart for Valentine Burke." *Moody Monthly.* February 1986, Page 120.

Bibliographical References

Romans 1:17: Voice on the Staircase

The World Almanac and Book of Facts. 1994. Mahwah, N. J.: Funk and Wagnalls, 1993. Page 727.

Douglas, J. D. and Philip W. Comfort, eds. *Who's Who in Christian History.* Wheaton, Ill.: Tyndale House Publishers, Inc., 1992. Page 433-437.

Watts, Dorothy Eaton. *This Is The Day.* Hagerstown, Md.: Review and Herald Pub. Assoc., 1982. Page 312.

Watts, Dorothy Eaton. *Stepping Stones.* Hagerstown, Md.: Review and Herald Pub. Assoc., 1987. Page 165.

White, Ellen G. *The Great Controversy.* Boise, Idaho: Pacific Press Pub. Assoc., 1939. Pages 120-170.

1 Corinthians 3:11: The Elect Lady

Boreham, F. W. *Life Verses.* Grand Rapids, Mich.: Kregel Publications, 1994. Volume 3, Pages 212-224.

Encyclopedia Britannica. Chicago, Ill.: William Benton, 1965. Volume 11, page 897.

Little, Bryan. *Selina, Countess of Huntingdon.* Bath, United Kingdom: The Huntingdon Centre, 1989. Page 20.

Tucker, Ruth and W. L. Liefeld. *Daughters of the Church.* Grand Rapids, Mich.: Zondervan Publishing House, 1987. Page 239.

1 Corinthians 3:12-14: Voice in the Wind

Houghton, Frank L. *Amy Carmichael of Dohnavur.* Fort Washington, Penn.: Christian Literature Crusade, 1953.

Skoglund, Elizabeth R. *Wounded Heroes.* Grand Rapids, Mich.: Baker Book House, 1992. Pages 63-82.

Spangler, Ann and Charles Turner, eds. *Heroes.* Ann Arbor, Mich.: Servant Publications, 1985. Pages 17-36.

Tucker, Ruth A. *Guardians of the Great Commission.* Grand Rapids, Mich.: Zondervan, 1988. Pages 130-135.

Watts, Dorothy Eaton. *The Best You Can Be.* Hagerstown, Md.: Review and Herald Pub. Assoc., 1993. Pages 29-31.

Woodbridge, John, ed. *More Than Conquerors.* Chicago, Ill.: Moody

Press, 1992. Pages 69-72.

Ephesians 4:17: Saved from Suicide

Landorf, Joyce. *His Stubborn Love.* Grand Rapids, Mich.: Zondervan Publishing House, 1971. Pages 62-73.
Heatherly, Joyce Landorf. *Unworld People.* Austin, Tex.: Balcony Publishing, 1987.

1 Timothy 1:15: A Fire in His Heart

Boreham, F. W. *Live Verses.* Grand Rapids, Mich.: Kregel Publications, 1994. Volume 1, pages 51-61.
Carlyle, R. M. and A. J. Carlyle. *Hugh Latimer.* London: Methuen and Co., 1899. Page 177.
Davies, R. E. *I Will Pour Out My Spirit.* Tunbridge Wells, U.K.: Monarch Publications, 1992. Page 63.
Douglas, J. D. and P. W. Comfort, eds. *Who's Who in Christian History,* Wheaton, Ill.: Tyndale House Publishers, 1993. Pages 84, 413.
Durant, Will and Ariel Durant. *The Reformation.* New York: Simon & Schuster, 1957. Pages 593-601.
Encyclopedia Britannica. Chicago, Ill.: William Benton, 1965. Pages 743, 744.
Stuart, Clara H. *Latimer: Apostle to the English.* Grand Rapids, Mich.: Zondervan. 1986.

Hebrews 13:13: The Father of Modern Missions

Boreham, F. W. *Life Verses.* Grand Rapids, Mich.: Kregel Publications, 1994. Volume 1, pages 161-172.
Cowart, John W. *People Whose Faith Got Them Into Trouble.* Downer's Grove, Ill.: InterVarsity Press, 1990. Pages 89-99.
Douglas, J. D. and P. W. Comfort, eds. *Who's Who in Christian History.* Wheaton, Ill.: Tyndale House Publishers, 1992. Pages 137, 138.
Encyclopedia Brittanica. Chicago, Ill.: William Benton, 1965. Volume 10, page 562.
Fisk, Samuel. *40 Fascinating Conversion Stories.* Grand Rapids, Mich.: Kregel Publications, 1993. Pages 31-36.

Bibliographical References

Howell, Clifford G. *The Advance Guard of Missions.* Mountain View, Calif.: Pacific Press Pub. Assoc., 1912. Pages 84-100.

Latourette, Kenneth Scott. *A History of the Expansion of Christianity.* Grand Rapids, Mich.: Zondervan Publishing House, 1970. Pages 66-69.

Tucker, Ruth. *From Jerusalem to Irian Jaya.* Grand Rapids, Mich.: Zondervan Publishing House, 1983. Pages 114-121.

Woodbridge, John, ed. *Ambassadors For Christ.* Chicago, Ill.: Moody Press, 1994. Pages 20-29, 342, 343.